Carola Benedetto   Luciana Ciliento

TRANSLATED BY
Antony Shugaar

STORIES FOR
KIDS WHO WANT
TO SAVE THE WORLD

ILLUSTRATED BY
Roberta Maddalena Bireau

TRIANGLE
SQUARE
books for young readers

SEVEN STORIES PRESS
New York · Oakland · London

A TRIANGLE SQUARE BOOK FOR YOUNG READERS
PUBLISHED BY SEVEN STORIES PRESS

Copyright © 2019, Luciano Ciliento and Carola Benedetto
English translation © 2021 by Antony Shugaar

First published in Italy by DeA Planeta, Milano
Published by arrangement with Walkabout Literary Agency

First English-language edition October 2021.

SEVEN STORIES PRESS
140 Watts Street
New York, NY 10013
www.sevenstories.com

College professors and high school and middle school teachers may
order free examination copies of Seven Stories Press titles.
To order, visit www.sevenstories.com or send a fax
on school letterhead to (212) 226-1411.

Library of Congress Cataloging-in-Publication Data has been applied for.
ISBN: 978-1-64421-086-4 (hardcover)
ISBN: 978-1-64421-087-1 (ebook)

ENGLISH EDITION DESIGN
Beth Kessler, Dror Cohen, and Stewart Cauley

PRINTED IN CHINA

9 8 7 6 5 4 3 2 1

Contents

CONTENTS

Introduction

We who stand on the earth feel it is enormous. Full of barriers, mountains, and borders. From space, however, it's a small, blue ball floating in the darkness—so beautiful and fragile that you're tempted to embrace and protect it.

This book came into being in order to tell the stories of women and men—each from a different part of the world and with a unique culture, nose and eyes, way of life, and family—who have loved the earth and fought to defend it. Defying fear and opposing opinions, and even risking their own lives, they were and remain on the front lines to save the earth from the recklessness and indifference of those who assume its resources are endless and from the arrogance of those who believe it belongs entirely to them.

Their stories are important because they show us that everything is interconnected. They show us what is possible. You can do your part regardless of what your family looks like, whom you choose to love, how well educated you are, and how rich, how young, how unconventional, or how utterly ordinary you are. Start with small, everyday things: limiting waste and consumption and respecting the natural resources that are the patrimony and heritage of each and every one of us, especially future generations.

INTRODUCTION

The earth should be loved and respected, as should every creature who inhabits it, whatever order or species they may belong to: plants, animals, or human beings. As for us humans, we are one large family, and we should be aware that we live in a shared space with finite resources. "Our house is on fire," Greta Thunberg says, and we need to understand that and act now.

Everyone is responsible for this small, blue ball. So, let's all join our protagonists in a big embrace.

THE LITTLE STORY OF

VANDANA SHIVA

We're all seeds

Vandana takes off her blue shoes, tosses them over the side of the rocking chair in which she's been curled up, and runs toward her big sister Mira, calling for her to come to the garden. Mira smiles and lets her little sister lead the way. Vandana moves along comfortably, leaping lightly over the rows of tomatoes and watermelon. Barefoot, she sinks her toes into the moist soil: she already knows where seeds have been sown and where the two girls can walk confidently instead. She clutches Mira's hand in one of hers and carries a little pink canvas bag in the other. Their father stitched it for her on the new sewing machine, and she then filled it with carrot seeds.

"First of all, we need to thank the earthworms. They plow the soil for us, softening it and bringing the oxygen that will nourish the carrots."

"First of all, we need to thank the earthworms. They plow the soil for us, softening it and bringing the oxygen that will nourish the carrots," she explains. Then she joins her hands together, and her voice merges with Mira's as they recite a mantra, a Hindu prayer.

Vandana and Mira lean down, bringing their lips close to the ground, asking the earth's permission to dig a furrow. In India, the earth is a goddess: she is sacred, and before treading on her or cutting into her, even if it's just a small hole to plant a seed, you must always ask for her permission and blessing.

Vandana closes her eyes. She works the soles of her feet into the soft soil. When she feels warmth flowing into her flesh, she knows that the goddess has answered. Then she opens her eyes and gently sticks her fingers into the crumbly dirt. She carefully digs a small, round hole.

"Just smell how sweet it is," she says to Mira, scooping up a handful of soil. Then she carves out another round hole. "This will help hold the water in when the ground is dry and also make sure there isn't too much water in the ground during the rainy season."

At this point, she opens the pink sack and takes out the seeds.

"I'm going to put in nine, because nine is a magic number."

Vandana lives in India, in the little village of Dehra Dun, at the foot of the Himalayas, with Mira; their brother, Kuldip; their mother and father; and a fantastic grandmother who cooks all sorts of delicacies.

Her father is a park ranger, and he often brings home tiger cubs. For the past several years he's been making clothes for the whole family on a sewing machine. He likes sewing, but that sewing machine represents something much bigger. It's a tool of freedom, as Gandhi taught all Indians—Gandhi is also known as "Mahatma," or "great soul," for his wisdom.

Without using weapons, Gandhi led India in its struggle for independence from the British Empire. He urged all Indians to spin cotton thread into cloth and make their own clothing. Then he marched with them to the sea to gather salt, so they no longer had to buy it from the British colonialists.

"Every time we put on a garment spun by an Indian, that Indian's family can buy what they need to live, and everyone is happier," Baba-ji often says. (*Baba-ji* means "Papa" in Hindi.) And this happiness, which multiplies like *laddus*—the mountains of round pastries that Grandmother makes with flour and melted butter—strikes Vandana as the most precious thing in the world.

Vandana's mother, a farmer, looks after cattle. Vandana adores all animals but she is bewitched by cows. They are white with large eyes rimmed in black, as if painted with *kajal*, and they seem to her like elegant, powerful ladies. As her mother puts the cows away in their stalls, Vandana, who wants to know the reason for everything, asks, "Why are cows sacred?"

"Because the vehicle of the powerful god Shiva is a bull, and cows give us everything we need to live," her mother replies.

"And what do we need to live?"

"Milk, which we foam to make ghee, the butter you like so much. Then we can use their dried dung, round as an enormous coin, to light the fires we use to cook and heat the house. Last of all, we use their wet manure to fertil-ize the fields where we grow onions, rice, and lentils."

Vandana listens carefully. She knows that all things are linked together; her grandmother always tells her

"And what do we need to live?"

so. That night, as she's falling asleep, she thinks back to all the things she's learned.

"Go to sleep, Vandana," whispers her grandmother, who has come to wish her good night.

VANDANA SHIVA

"I'm not sleepy, Nani-ji"—which means something roughly equivalent to "Beloved-Grandma-Who-Is-So-Wise." "Will you tell me the story of the trees and the women?"

> A long time ago, in northern India, there lived a maharaja, a very cruel and arrogant king.

"I told it you yesterday, and the day before, too."

"I know, Nani-ji, but it's like your fritters. I never get tired of them."

And so, her grandmother, who can never say no to Vandana's big, dark eyes, starts telling the story:

A long time ago, in northern India, there lived a maharaja, a very cruel and arrogant king. During one especially hot and muggy summer, he was seized by the desire to stroll among refreshing fountains. And in the merest blink of an eye, he ordered his servants to chop down the entire forest around his palace and turn it into a garden full of tinkling water. But the news of this development reached the ears of Amrita Devi, a girl from a neighboring village, who immediately hurried over to defend the trees.

"Trees are precious. They protect animals, and with their roots they store the water that helps nourish the fields," she told the maharaja's servants, who were already hard at work chopping away.

The servants laughed heartily and started sawing branches off the first tree.

"Trees are sacred. When there is a drought and we have no food, we women come here to gather good herbs, and we use them to feed our families," Amrita insisted.

"Now you'll have to go somewhere else. We're building fountains for the maharaja here. Leave, return to your village on the double!" the servants yelled at her.

But Amrita ignored them and instead stepped forward.

This was the part that Vandana liked best, because she wouldn't have retreated a single step before such blatant injustice.

Amrita walked right up to the tallest tree and hugged it tightly, as if it were her brother or her mother.

"Kill her!" shouted the cruel maharaja, who had arrived in the forest in the meantime. And seeing that the servants lacked the courage to do it, he killed her himself. But no sooner had he killed her than every one of the other women ran to hug a tree. Ten, fifty, a hundred. The terrible maharaja killed many of them, but other women arrived from every corner of the kingdom. And when there were more than three hundred of them, the horrendous king finally put down his sword and trudged, defeated, back to his palace.

"The forest was saved thanks to the courage of Amrita Devi and the other women, isn't that right Nani-ji?"
"True, my little one. The courage of women knows

> "True, my little one. The courage of women knows no obstacles."

no obstacles. They're powerful, they embody Shakti, the female energy that creates worlds. And you are a woman; don't you ever forget it." Vandana nods and hugs her grandmother tight, feeling as safe as the trees in the story, and finally falls asleep.

The years go by, as fast as trains, and Vandana grows up. Soon she finds herself faced with her first adult choices and an important journey.

"Go on. Do what you think best," Baba-ji tells her after she finishes high school. And Vandana, who has never stopped trying to understand the reasons for things, plunges into the study of physics, and eventually sets out for one of the best universities in the world, the University of Guelph, in Ontario, Canada.

Baba-ji and Mata-ji—*Mata-ji* means "Mama" in Hindi—want nothing but the best for their children. Unlike the parents of many of her girlfriends, they don't care if Vandana finds a husband or a traditional job.

"Vandana, there's only one thing that I want, now and always," Baba-ji tells her, looking her right in the eye. "I always want you to be free and courageous like Mahatma Gandhi. Remember, there is no arrogant bully who can't be stopped by firm determination. Will you do your best?"

"Yes, I promise you I will. I'll learn everything there

> "I want all Indian children to study, but more important, to eat good food and breathe clean air. There's a lot of work to be done!"

is to learn, but I'll certainly come home again. I want all Indian children to study, but more important, to eat good food and breathe clean air. There's a lot of work to be done!" she replies, excited now, while Mata-ji, trying to distract herself from a surging feeling of sadness, helps her pack the enormous suitcase with clothing, spices, pastries from her grandmother, and family pictures.

When she returns home for her summer vacation, Vandana realizes that something's getting worse in India. All over the country, the forests are being thinned and beaten back. Trees are being chopped down to be sold for lumber and so that minerals can be mined from the depths of the earth. With encroaching deforestation, life in the villages is getting more and more difficult. More and more families are being forced out in search of new land; poor children beg on the streets. And so, Vandana joins the many women of the Chipko Andolan, a movement whose participants hug trees in order to protect them, in memory of Amrita Devi. In the end, the Indian government recognizes their concerns: the forests will be protected to ensure that they continue to offer a source of livelihood, and India's villages survive.

After the University of Guelph, Vandana goes on to pursue graduate studies in quantum physics at the University of Western Ontario, where she delves into the invisible structure of matter.

When she finally comes back to Dehra Dun, to live in the village for good, in 1978, a grand festival of celebration takes place there. Relatives and friends come from the surrounding villages to see her, to drink chai (a spicy black tea with milk) and eat *laddus* and fritters.

The next morning, Vandana takes a drive toward the mountain with Mira. They drive down the road that runs alongside the forest, the way they did when they

"It's time to rediscover the strength and courage of Amrita Devi."

were little girls in search of cool shade and aromatic herbs. That's when Vandana sees with her own eyes the trunks of thousands of giant oak trees that have been felled. This is the work of mining companies who want to facilitate access for their dump trucks loaded with rocks. For a moment, she can't breathe, and she comes close to crying.

"It's time to rediscover the strength and courage of Amrita Devi, time to do my best to get things back to the way they ought to be," she tells herself at last, with determination.

Now Vandana works at the Indian Institute of Management Bangalore, where she is undertaking a research project on the damage that the recent transformation of farms into eucalyptus plantations has done to the region. There she discovers that science and technology are often used for negative objectives. The World Bank, in fact, has financed the eucalyptus plantation project, describing it as a form of reforestation, a positive effort meant to bring trees back to areas that have been clear-cut. However, planting thousands of trees of the same species has impoverished the natural environment, making it more vulnerable to wildfires. What's more, the eucalyptus tree wasn't chosen because it is well suited to that location, but because its fiber is perfect for making paper: again, the aim of the project was only to make money.

The more she learns, the more Vandana feels an urgent need to devote all her time and effort to defending the earth. In order to do that, however, she has to be free, "like Gandhi, who owed nothing to anyone," as Baba-ji would have said. So, she quits her job and decides that, from that day on, she's going to be an independent scientist and not work for the government, whose documents are, perhaps, only half true anyway.

In her parents' stables, she starts the Research Foundation for Science, Technology, and Ecology, a center for the study of biodiversity (the variety of living organisms inhabiting our planet) but also the environmental impact of dams and hydroelectric power stations on nature.

First, she looks into the Narmada River, in central India. The course of the river, one of India's most sacred, has been altered, rerouted by thousands of obstructions and dams to make use of waterpower and to extract precious metals for manufacturing. Vandana and her new colleagues gather information, testimonies, and documents, and they soon discover that the situation is dire—especially around the limestone quarries of the Doon Valley. There's a shortage of water and food for people and pasturage for animals. It's not

VANDANA SHIVA

even possible to find lumber to build houses, because the forests have vanished. What's more, during the pounding monsoon rains, the rubble from the excavations, piled up around the quarries, is swept into the riverbed. As a result, the river overflows, and villages are flooded.

"The companies you're fighting are very powerful. You can't hope to win!" people often tell Vandana, but she won't give up. And the inhabitants of the towns along the Narmada River and the women of the Chipko movement are by her side protesting, too.

After a hundred days of protests and struggles, Van-

> "The companies you're
> fighting are very powerful.
> You can't hope to win!"

dana is summoned by the highest court in India, the Supreme Court. In the end, the truth wins out: "The mines of the Doon Valley will be shut down!" the presiding judge decrees, slamming down his gavel.

That night, tired but happy, Vandana tells Baba-ji about the verdict. "Certainly, there's no standing in the way of progress," she concludes, searching again for comfort in her father's deep, wise eyes, "but you can't destroy everything, either! You understand,

Baba-ji, this is only one of the many battles that lie ahead for us!"

Vandana knows that big multinational corporations have come to India to sell genetically modified seeds. These GMO seeds—seeds produced in laboratories with modified DNA—aren't natural, and they ruin the soil and impoverish the farmlands. The companies are promising Indian farmers miraculous harvests. In reality, though, as soon as there's a drought, the plants sprouting from these new seeds are bound to die, and then the farmers will find themselves starting over from scratch: buying new seeds at ever-higher prices in an endless, escalating spiral.

"They've even tried to modify the basmati rice that has been growing in our valleys for centuries, going so far as to claim that they invented it. You can't invent a seed! No one invents seeds, and no one owns them," Vandana says, increasingly indignant.

"The situation is frightening," Baba-ji replies. "These are seeds that give big harvests the first year and then gradually leach the nutrients from the soil, leaving it barren. If you want to make it fertile again, you need pesticides, chemical products sold by the same companies, stuff that will poison the earth. Many farmers have lost everything and been driven to suicide."

"I need to do something!" Vandana says. "I'm a scientist, and I feel responsible for this disaster caused by

VANDANA SHIVA

other scientists. I need to find a solution. And if there isn't one in everything I've studied so far, I'll find it somewhere else!"

The solution is right under her eyes or, actually, right under her window: in the old vegetable garden in her backyard—in caring for the earth, in asking her permission to plant seeds and sprouts, in thanking her for the food she so generously gives us.

This is the turning point. Vandana founds the Navdanya Seed Bank—*Navdanya* means "nine seeds" but also "new gift"—with Bija Devi, a woman farmer and friend. (*Bija* means, appropriately enough, "seed.") According to Hindu astrology, the nine seeds also represent the planets, because the earth is not alone, and everything, even humans, exists in relation to the cosmos.

"You must always enter the seed room barefoot, because seeds are sacred, and life depends on them," Bija Devi likes to say. Together, the two women harvest age-old,

> The solution is right under her eyes or, actually, right under her window: in the old vegetable garden in her backyard.

natural seeds from their fields, instead of the genetically modified ones, and donate them to the local farmers.

Five years later, the Seed Bank becomes a full-fledged farm, the Navdanya Farm, where more than six hundred varieties of vegetables and medicinal herbs are raised alongside over two hundred varieties of rice. Five years after that comes the founding of Bija Vidyapeeth, its name meaning "Seed University." A site for conferences on organic farming techniques and natural insecticides, it is also there to remind us that food is sacred and gives us the gift of life.

Today, Navdanya is an international network of seed custodians and organic farmers spread out over more than twenty-two Indian states. To date, Navdanya has helped found 124 seed banks housing collections of "spontaneous seeds," kept not in safes but in countless small vases, each with a label bearing the seed's name. Thanks to Vandana's courage, a community of people who respect the earth has come into being, people who have rescued and protected thousands of plants.

"Preserving seeds means preserving biodiversity and the knowledge and culture of all humanity," Vandana never tires of saying, at Navdanya and around the world.

THE LITTLE STORY OF
RACHEL CARSON

Spring won't be silent anymore

L ittle Rachel studies the robin that has just alighted on the windowsill of her home in Springdale, Pennsylvania. For the past two days, the bird has made its appearance at lunchtime, when the sun is at its warmest and the icy winter wind loosens its iron grip. It perches there gently on its slender legs. Motionless, it stares at her. Then it hops forward. A clump of snow falls and lands, wet and heavy, on the sidewalk below. The robin seems ready to fly away, but instead of spreading its wings, it stops and pecks at the seeds Rachel has set out in a pile. After it's done eating, it takes flight.

You are the springtime, Rachel thinks. Then she pulls away from the pane of glass and runs outside. She studies the sky for the robin and finds it flying up to the highest branch of an oak tree. Season after season, Rachel—who is ten years old now—has learned that when the robin arrives, winter comes to an end and spring slowly covers the fields with green, fills the

flower beds with blooms and the air with the buzz-
ing of insects and the chirping of birds. She's an acute
observer, and spring is the time of year she loves best,
because everything is teeming with life. Soon she'll be
able to wander over the family farm, through woods,
fruit orchards, and fields along the Allegheny River,
observing insect life, discovering the burrows of wild
hares and raccoons, and recognizing birds by their
song. Her mother, Maria, is a musician, so Rachel has
refined her sense of hearing by listening to her at the
piano. She can easily identify the species of bird from
the sound of its chirping.

> "The woods are calling me,"
> she tells her mother. Looking out the
> window, she asks, "Can I go?"

Early one March morning, Rachel comes running down
the wooden staircase and sits down at the kitchen table.
"I dreamt I was having lunch with Beatrix Potter's rab-
bits! And there were ladybirds inviting me to go outside
with them. . . . The woods are calling me," she tells her
mother. Looking out the window, she asks, "Can I go?"
Her mother, who always encourages her to cultivate her
passions and is convinced that the first and best teacher

in life is nature, smiles as she puts together a basket with a large slice of pie and a bottle of milk.

"Keep your neck nice and warm; the spring air is chilly," she replies as she hands Rachel the basket.

Rachel is beaming. In less than five minutes her silhouette can be seen running into the woods, accompanied by her dog. Behind them, in the moist soil, one can see a double track of footprints and pawprints.

Down a path running between the white elms, the scent of moss and daisies in the air, Rachel reaches a burrow of wild hares. Indifferent to her white stockings, which are getting permanently stained, she gets down on all fours to try to see a hare poking out its head, with her dog waiting in ambush beside her. But just as a hare is about to emerge, she hears a robin sing and leaps to her feet. In response, her companion barks, and the little hare hurries back underground. The bird flaps its wings and vanishes.

"Are you the one who was eating from my windowsill? Come on, let me take a look at you," Rachel pleads with the bird, which is already gone, heading who knows where. In a few seconds she also makes out the call of a thrush and even the song of a rare yellowthroat. The woods are a symphony of notes and trills. Rachel is captivated.

She sits on a rounded rock and takes out the slice of her mother's pie. As the crumbs fall to the ground, they attract a line of ants, and the sweet filling brings over a bee that buzzes around her with its dull, droning sound. *Insects are highly intelligent,* she thinks as she watches the ants' incessant, hardworking comings and goings. Rachel can see that nature is not only beautiful, but also a sort of a great, overarching alchemy, where everything is connected: the presence of insects is necessary for the birds, for instance, but also crucial in terms of the pollination of flowers, as her mother explained to her, showing her the bees hard at work in the fruit orchard.

As she heads home, she feels as if she has just witnessed a magnificent spectacle. Her eyes are satiated and her mouth rich with descriptions to tell her mother and to note down on paper. Writing and reading are two other important passions for Rachel, who not only studies hard at school, sparing no effort, but also reads on her own, taking on increasingly complex and challenging books, such as the exotic seafaring adventures of Joseph Conrad, Herman Melville, and Robert Louis Stevenson. At the young age of eleven, taking inspiration from a story she heard from her brother, who was in the military, Rachel writes a short story about a courageous pilot in the Royal Flying Corps. She titles it, "A Battle in the Clouds," and sends it to the children's publication *St. Nicholas Magazine,* of which she is a loyal reader. One afternoon, she receives a letter: the story has been awarded a Silver Badge, a small cash prize, and is going to be published. With the letter still clutched tightly in her hand, Rachel runs over to her mother sitting before the piano and excitedly announces, "I'm going to be a writer!" The following year, another short story wins the Golden Badge, an even higher award. And many other stories follow, nourishing her dream.

But these are tough years for dreamers, because the economic downturn is getting worse. Her parents make many sacrifices: her father is a traveling salesman, and her mother is a piano teacher; she sells chickens and apples to make ends meet. They need money to supplement Rachel's scholarship, so she can attend the Pennsylvania College for Women, in Pittsburgh. They spend months scrimping and saving, in addition to selling the family's porcelain. One morning, Rachel hops into a rented Model T and takes off for her new life.

While she's away at school, things get worse at home. When she returns for summer vacation, she finds her sister is divorced, her brother is out of work, and the countryside is gray with soot from the smokestacks of nearby factories, as industry grows wildly. Rachel is tempted to run away, partly because her home is filled with sad faces and partly because she has the feeling that nature is being ravaged by a ravenous predator, pollution.

RACHEL CARSON

She senses that there's still very little she can do for her family, but maybe she can do something for the environment. To learn more, once she's back in college, she sneaks into a biology lesson being taught by Professor Mary Scott Skinker, just the professor says, "Women can study to become scientists, exactly like men. It's time for things to change. Let's get to work." Rachel remains for the rest of the class. For the first time, she glimpses the possibility of dedicating herself professionally to the things she loves best. At age twenty-one, she changes from studying English literature to biology, though she is often criticized for choosing what was then considered a masculine profession.

In a letter to her mother, she writes, "I know that you're worried and that the rumors that reach you are spiteful. Don't worry, though, I know what I'm doing. For that matter, as a writer, I've never had that much imagination. At last, now, plants, animals, and their wonderful connections will provide me with countless plots. After all, you're the one who taught me that nature is the best teacher."

Increasingly determined, Rachel spends that summer at the Marine Biological Laboratory in Woods Hole,

"Women can study to become scientists, exactly like men. It's time for things to change."

Massachusetts. For the first time, her eyes are filled with the impetuous ocean waters, and she is stunned by the marine ecosystem, an array of birds, seaweed, and fish.

Science becomes her life, and in a few years' time, Rachel completes a master of science degree in zoology and genetics at Johns Hopkins University, with a specialty in marine biology.

In the meantime, the economic downturn in the United States has reached its climax. This is the Great Depression. And to an even greater degree after her father's death, there isn't enough money to support the family, with her mother, sister, and two nephews all living together in her new home in Maryland. While she works for the *Baltimore Sun*, she also teaches part time at the university to make ends meet and applies for still other jobs. When she's under too much pressure, she goes out and walks alone for hours. She seeks out the comfort of nature as well as good ideas to improve the situation.

She finally gets a job with the U.S. Bureau of Fisheries. She writes copy for a series of radio shorts called *Romance Under the Waters*. The program is a hit. The following year, she does brilliantly on the government scientist test and finds work as a biologist with the Fisheries Bureau, the second woman in the whole country, again.

In 1941, she publishes her first book devoted to life in the oceans, *Under the Sea Wind: A Naturalist's Picture of*

Ocean Life. The book gives her new credibility and fame as an author and scientist. In a short time, she becomes the editor in chief of all the bureau's publications—a rare thing for a woman in this period. Ten years later, she publishes her second book, *The Sea Around Us*, in which she lays out the importance of the oceans, their hidden canyons, the effects of winds, and the relationship between human beings and the sea over the centuries. So many copies of the book are sold that in the following years, she quits her job so she can devote herself full time to research and writing. The product of this is *The Edge of the Sea*, the book that concludes her marine trilogy.

One January afternoon in 1958, Rachel receives a copy of a letter her friend Olga Owens Huckins sent to the *Boston Herald*. Olga lives near a marshy area in Massachusetts where the state is conducting a campaign to rid the area of mosquitoes by spraying DDT from airplanes. She wrote the following after finding over a dozen dead birds near her home:

> All of these birds died horribly, and in the same way. Their bills gaping open, and their splayed claws were drawn up to their breasts in agony. The remedy of this situation is not to double the strength of the spray and come again. It is to STOP THE SPRAYING OF POISONS FROM THE AIR everywhere until all the evidence, biological and scientific, immediate

and long run, of the effects [of DDT] upon wildlife and human beings are known.

Rachel is stunned. She's determined to find out more. She reaches out to other scientists and learns that, in the South, cases like the one Olga described are legion. From Mississippi to Louisiana and all the way to Alabama, entire regions have been virtually stripped of their birds. The fruit the birds usually eat is left to rot on the branches, and the seeds left out in bowls remain uneaten for weeks at a time. The citizens are frightened by an unsettling silence: no birdsong.

What strikes Rachel with particular force is what's

> The citizens are frightened by an unsettling silence: no birdsong.

happened to her beloved robins in the city of East Lansing, Michigan. A fungus threatened the white elm trees, a favorite habitat for these birds, and the city sprayed the trees with DDT. In just a few months, the university grounds became a robin graveyard. What happened? The pesticide, sprayed in large volume, coated the leaves and the bark with a film that not even the rains were capable of removing. When the leaves fell in autumn and rotted into mulch, the earthworms ate it. And then, in springtime, when the robins flew north again and ate the earthworms, they were poisoned and died.

"It only takes eleven contaminated earthworms to effectively kill a robin. Robins eat approximately that much in as many minutes. The robin made up only a small part of the chain. Mortality rates rose among ninety different species of birds. Mammals, such as raccoons, shrews, and opossums that ate earthworms as well were also affected."

But the damage also comes from the agricultural pesticides applied in massive doses to preserve crops. Washed away by the rains, they reach the rivers and also poison the fish. The poisons thus enter the food chain, affecting all orders of creatures, up to and including humans, who fish and nourish themselves on the products of the soil.

She confides in great alarm to her mother over a hot cup of tea, "There are even traces of pesticides in mother's milk!"

Her mother replies in a worried tone, "You're about to uncover a kettle full of trouble. You'd better be careful . . ."

"I can't remain silent. I have to denounce the systematic poisoning that human beings are inflicting on their own environment. I'm an independent scientist—there is no lobby paying for my research—so I have to tell the truth. I know that the chemical industries are very

RACHEL CARSON

powerful and that they won't think twice about smearing me," she concludes, drinking her last gulp of tea.

Certain about the right thing to do, Rachel assembles her discoveries into a book that will soon overwhelm public opinion in America and around the world. The book is *Silent Spring*, an appalling vision of a world without birds. The intention of this book is to awaken people's understanding of the fact that everything is connected and intertwined and that certain human actions that might perhaps seem harmless, such as removing a fungus from trees, can actually cause incalculable damage and unthinkable imbalances.

"When you eliminate an insect entirely, for instance, you alter a balance, that ability nature has to self-regulate by virtue of the proper presence of predators and prey. The result is that you thus obtain an exponential increase in the presence of other insects or animals, triggering further problems," Rachel jots down on the book's galleys.

These concepts were already well known to science, and Rachel denounced them forcefully, assembling them in a single book complete with clear and unmistakable proof. As expected, with the publication of *Silent Spring* in 1962, lobbyists for the chemical industries react violently. They launch a quarter-million-dollar campaign to discredit Rachel, both as a scientist and a woman. The mass media depict her as follows: "She's nothing but a hysterical, unmarried, childless woman." And they promote poison use: "Without pesticides, we'd be overrun by insects and there wouldn't be enough food for us to eat." Actually, Rachel isn't calling for the total abandonment of chemical pesticides. She is in favor of regulating and moderating their use, in light of the harmful effects being documented.

So great is the uproar triggered by the book that Presi-

Spring won't be silent anymore.

dent John F. Kennedy asks the department in charge of these issues, the Office of Science and Technology, to investigate. The OST eventually confirms the accuracy of the scientist's findings. In just a few years, new laws are passed to protect the environment. What's more, the Environmental Protection Agency (EPA), a federal government agency, is established to ensure the protection of the environment and human health—and the use of DDT is gradually restricted in the United States. *Silent Spring* sells millions of copies around the world, inspiring the worldwide spread of environmental movements.

Rachel has won: she's proven to everyone that poisoning nature means poisoning ourselves. In the meantime, she's fallen sick with cancer, though she goes on working right up to the end, always smiling and recounting the wonders of nature.

On the day that Rachel Carson dies, April 14, 1964, a robin sits on her windowsill singing sweetly, as if to thank her for the handful of seeds she takes care to leave out every day, just as she did when she was a girl. Rachel smiles and thinks, *Spring won't be silent anymore.*

RACHEL CARSON

THE LITTLE STORY OF

DIAN FOSSEY

Gorillas are my family

Her house is too quiet, and Dian is always outside playing with the neighbors' dogs. She likes animals, maybe more than people, and with dogs, she never feels she's being judged; nor does she have to engage in lengthy conversations. She'd like to have a dog all her own, but her mother is dead set against it. And her stepfather is even stricter: he orders Dian to eat in the kitchen with the housekeeper. "Children get bored in the dining room," he says. In reality, only he gets bored.

When she turns seventeen, she can finally go to college.

"I choose veterinary science," Dian says, hoping that will mean she'll be surrounded by lots of animals all day long.

Her stepfather interrupts, impatient: "You don't have any money of your own, and we're paying your tuition. You'll go to business school."

Dian detests arithmetic and numbers, but she has no alternative.

During her summer vacations, she works on a farm, doing just about everything. Surrounded by rolling green fields and lakes, she has the time of her life with the cattle and the horses. What's more, her time there allows her to sock away sufficient savings to quit business school and enroll in school for veterinary science. Dian is an outstanding student in all subjects that have to do with animals, but she really shows no gift for other fields, such as chemistry and physics. So, in the end, she quits school.

In 1954, she takes a degree in occupational therapy and immediately finds a job in a hospital in Kentucky, where she cares for children on the autism spectrum. While she's there, she rents an old cottage on a big farm just outside Louisville. When they find out she studied veterinary science, the owners of the farm ask her to look after the animals. Dian wakes up to the mooing of cows, takes care of the horses, and then goes to the hospital to care for her children.

One evening after work, she meets a young man who lived in Africa for many years. He tells her all about his experiences, and suggests, "If you like animals, that's the place for you!"

Dian listens to him in rapt fascination. She wants to go, no matter the cost. Africa becomes an obsession for her and, doing a thousand extra odd jobs, she manages to scrape together enough money for the plane ticket. In the meantime, she reads travel literature, African history, and zoology books. One evening, she happens upon a copy of *The Year of the Gorilla,* by George Schaller, an American zoologist who studied these mammals in Cameroon and the Congo. She devours the book in a single night, and the next morning at dawn, she decides, *I'm going to go find gorillas.*

"Are you crazy? They're really dangerous," her friend responds when she tells him of her plan.

I'm going to go find gorillas.

"Schaller describes them as shy, gentle creatures. I'm not afraid. I'm going to go the Congo, to the Virunga Mountains, and I'll study them there," Dian decides.

She plans her trip down to the smallest detail: on her first stop, she's going to meet the paleoanthropologist and archaeologist Louis Leakey, who studies primates and supports young researchers who want to follow in his footsteps.

In 1963, she flies to Africa for the very first time. She meets Leakey in Tanzania. Though enthusiastic about Dian's planned studies, he worries that a young woman all alone and without experience is not going to be able to withstand the exhausting demands that such study will entail. Soon enough, he realizes he has underestimated her.

Dian glimpses six dark, enormous silhouettes.

In fact, Dian hires a team of porters to help her carry everything she's going to need to set up camp, and after just two weeks, she reaches the slopes of Mount Mikeno, Schaller's old base of operations. At an elevation of three thousand meters, in the midst of unspoiled nature shrouded in fog, she feels right at home. Not far off, she spots a pair of American photographers. They are also on the lookout for gorillas, so the two groups join forces.

For days they see nothing—until, one morning, they catch a whiff of an acrid odor.

Suddenly, the silence of the mountains is shattered by a dull, persistent noise: the sound of gorillas beating their chests. Dian glimpses six dark, enormous silhouettes.

She is struck by their dark, gleaming, intense eyes. The males, bigger, are in the front line; the females, for their part, remain off to one side and never lose track of their young. The gorillas' "troop" leader takes a threatening stance while observing Dian and the photographers. When the photographers turn the movie camera on and steer it toward the gorillas, they fall silent as they listen to the faint whirr of the camera's motor. Then the troop leader yawns. At that sign, the whole troop relaxes and starts to interact with the camera: one gorilla starts circling around it; another walks shyly in front of it; and still others challenge it, baring their teeth.

Each one has his or her own personality, Dian thinks when the troop of gorillas scatters into the forest.

Her first trip to Africa ends without any other sightings. Dian is determined to head back to America, but only long enough to organize a new trip to study gorillas.

She writes many articles about Africa, and a small newspaper publishes them, dubbing her the "gorilla lady." Unexpectedly, Professor Leakey delivers a lecture in that same period, in Louisville. Dian is eager to say hello to him, and remembering Dian and her courage perfectly, Leakey asks her, "Would you come back to Africa? I need someone willing to study the gorillas for years, and you seem just crazy enough . . ."

Each one has his or her own personality.

41

"When do I leave?" Dian replies, already imagining herself back among the mountain mists.

"In eight months. We have funding from the National Geographic Society," Leakey explains.

And so, in the winter of 1966, Dian is back on a plane heading for Africa. She lands in Nairobi and buys everything she's going to need for her camp: sleeping mats, durable tents for herself and her porters, blankets and camp stoves. Then she travels a thousand kilometers by car, to Virunga National Park, in the Congo. Covering a diverse array of highlands, precipices, gorges, forests, and plains, the national park extends over the slopes of eight volcanoes and crosses the borders of three African nations: Democratic Republic of the Congo, Rwanda, and Uganda. When they reach the clearing of Kabara, they set up the camp from which they will set out every day to do their research.

> **"The troop is a sort of family formed by about ten gorillas, headed by a male silverback, at least twice the size of the others."**

Dian quickly learns to recognize the tracks left by passing gorillas. She studies their footprints, the food dropped uneaten, the "nests" they build as beds for the night or shelters from the rain, and even their stool.

After several weeks, she finally discovers a recent trail. At a certain point, she hears the gorillas' calls and spots the first troop from a distance, with a telescope. She follows them for many days. One evening in her tent, her clothing still wet, and by the light of a kerosene lamp, she writes, "The troop is a sort of family formed by about ten gorillas, headed by a male silverback, at least twice the size of the others."

And she starts to give distinctive names to each gorilla, identifying them by the pattern of wrinkles above their nostrils.

It takes months before the gorillas accept her constant presence. To avoid frightening them, Dian never stands up, and she is very careful not to run. Usually, she approaches them on all fours and then lies down on her belly, a gesture of submission. Often, to arouse their curiosity, she will imitate them: sometimes she scratches her head, pretends to eat leaves, or climbs trees as best she can. And they seem to enjoy watching, very much.

Now the primates of Virunga trust her, and soon Dian has irrefutable evidence of this fact. One day, a student who has only recently joined the crew of observers approaches a gorilla family too quickly. Right away, the dominant male runs at him fast, ready to chase away someone he considers an enemy. Dian lunges past the young man, pushing him to the ground as she does.

As soon as he sees her, the male gorilla stops, calming down immediately.

That evening, Dian makes an entry: "I learned to accept the animals on their own terms and never to push them beyond the varying levels of tolerance they were willing to give. Any observer is an intruder in the domain of a wild animal and must remember that the rights of that animal supersede human interests."

A few days later, farther downhill, clashes break out between two provinces of the Congolese region of Kivu. Dian realizes what's going on only when a detachment of soldiers surrounds the camp and takes her to the town of Rumangabo, where they put her under lock and key "for her own safety." She remains a prisoner for two weeks, until she tricks her captors into releasing her and escapes across the border into neighboring Uganda. As a researcher, she wants to get straight back to work, but her tools are in the Congo now, and she can't go back to get them because she's a prison escapee. Luckily, with the help of Professor Leakey and the National Geographic Society, she is able to buy new materials,

"Any observer is an intruder in the domain of a wild animal and must remember that the rights of that animal supersede human interests."

and she goes back to Virunga National Park, but this time on the Rwandan side.

And so, in September 1967, in a valley between Mount Karisimbi and Mount Visoke, Dian sets up her new camp, which she calls Karisoke, and sets out in search of gorillas again.

One morning, she meets a young gorilla she'll come to love very much. He's a young male, and as his group moves away, he turns to look at her, as if undecided. Dian notices that he has a crooked finger, and so she names him Digit.

A few weeks later, she encounters another group, and something extraordinary happens. A young gorilla gazes at her kindly. "You're Peanuts," she tells him in a soft voice, careful not to scare him away. And Peanuts doesn't move. In fact, every time they meet, he stops to look at her, lingering a little longer. One day, he comes very

> Dian notices that he has a crooked finger, and so she names him Digit.

close, just a few steps away, while Dian pretends to chew some leaves and scratches her head to reassure him. Peanuts imitates her. So, Dian lies flat on the ground and slowly extends her hand, palm turned upward.

The gorilla, too, lies down, and their fingers brush, intertwining in the end. At that point, Peanuts suddenly leaps to his feet and pounds his chest, but this time for joy.

Dian, too, is in seventh heaven. This is the first time she's touched a gorilla. She feels a profound love for these creatures and perceives their vulnerability in a world that considers them to be little more than curiosities. In that contact, she makes a pact with them: she'll defend them, whatever the cost.

In fact, on her way home, she notices that the forest is riddled with traps set by poachers. Even though it's a nature preserve, the park has become prime poaching territory. The poachers catch and kill antelopes, water buffalos, wild boars, and—less frequently—gorillas, whose heads and paws are sold on the black market as ashtrays for tourists.

> With her African coworkers and her foreign students, Dian organizes the first antipoaching teams.

With her African coworkers and her foreign students, Dian organizes the first antipoaching teams. They trigger the traps and remove them. When they can't remove them all in time, they chase away the approaching gorillas, using the "herding" technique: they ring poacher dog bells, or bells just like the ones they've confiscated from the poachers' dogs. It's a traumatic technique for the primates, and when the gorillas run away, they emit the acrid odor of fear, leaving behind obvious trails of excrement and blood. To keep the gorillas from having to be subjected to this ordeal, Dian confronts the poachers openly, trying to persuade them to leave the gorillas alone. She knows that most of the poachers are poor, and she often recruits them to work in her antipoaching teams, provided they agree to give up poaching. Dian never keeps a penny of her funds for herself. Despite her commitment, the gorillas remain in danger.

One day, the park conservator comes up to the camp. "The Cologne Zoological Garden wants a mountain gorilla. In exchange, they'll give us a Land Rover and money for the park," he announces, as if this were an acceptable exchange.

"But if you want to capture one, you have to kill the whole family, because they'll try to defend it," Dian retorts, aghast.

"Well, if you won't help us, we'll do it on our own!" These are his parting words.

Of course, Dian doesn't help them. And six months later, when the conservator summons her urgently to his office, she discovers that they've done exactly what they threatened to do: a young gorilla, undernourished and beaten up, is looking out at her miserably from a small cage where it's been confined for weeks now.

"You need to take care of it," the man orders Dian. "In this condition, it will never survive the journey to the zoo."

The suffering of that poor creature takes Dian's breath away and causes her to think about the pain that human beings cause without a second thought.

Dismayed, Dian takes the wounded animal back to the encampment. She arranges a room with leaves and sticks of wood. Then she readies food and medicines. When the little gorilla steps out of the cage, it cries like a human baby. The suffering of that poor creature takes Dian's breath away and causes her to think about the pain that human beings cause without a second thought. She names the young gorilla Coco. And she does everything she can to care for her and set her free as quickly as possible.

Unfortunately, the unhappy surprises aren't over. Just a few days later, another young gorilla, a female, newly captured, is brought to the camp in a sad condition. After two weeks of loving care and treatment, the second young gorilla, whom Dian names Pucker, recovers. Soon, the two young gorillas spend their days playing together, running at breakneck speed around the clearing, tormenting the hens, jumping onto the dog's back, and taking apart anything they can get their hands on, until they finally fall fast asleep, exhausted, their arms wrapped around each other.

I'll never again give in to requests that might endanger the gorillas' lives, Dian promises herself.

When the conservator returns to send the young gorillas off to Cologne, Dian stalls for time. The man threatens to have other gorillas captured, and she gives in, remembering that ten gorillas were killed to catch Coco. Two months later, she receives a letter stating that the little one let itself starve to death at the zoo.

I'll never again give in to requests that might endanger the gorillas' lives, Dian promises herself.

In the years that follow, more gorillas are killed, including her beloved Digit. Dian creates the "Digit Fund" to raise money to combat poaching and try to keep tourists and rubberneckers far away from the gorillas. But it isn't easy. The government realizes that the public's desire to see animals in the wild is a huge source of revenue, and

> "The man who kills the animals today
> is the man who kills the people
> who get in his way tomorrow."

so they allow ever greater numbers of people to access the park without imposing any rules on them regarding respecting nature and the animals. Dian knows that she alone can't make a difference, and that the Africans themselves have to love and protect their land. And so, she involves and trains growing numbers of locals, urging them to protect the gorillas and their habitat. Naturally, by doing this, she makes plenty of enemies.

In December 1985, Dian is found dead in her cabin, mysteriously murdered.

She was right when she said, "The man who kills the animals today is the man who kills the people who get in his way tomorrow."

Now she is buried next to Digit. In her honor, the Dian Fossey Fund is established for the protection of gorillas, and her love for animals still protects them today.

THE LITTLE STORY OF
AL GORE

The truth
is inconvenient

lbert Gore Jr. is a sensible young man who asks his parents a seemingly endless stream of questions, including on grown-up subjects. He has just realized that his country, the United States, is undergoing a complicated era when a new piece is added to the jigsaw puzzle of reality he is discovering. He has only recently turned fourteen when, one late-summer evening, his mother summons him and his sister to the kitchen of their farmhouse in Carthage, Tennessee, where the family spends summer vacation. She wants to show them something truly important: Rachel Carson's *Silent Spring*, a book that lays out the harmful effects of the chemical pesticides and insecticides so popular then. The book is revolutionary for its time, to put it mildly, because in the sixties no one is interested in slowing down agricultural or industrial production or cutting profits in order to prevent pollution. Their mother, who has a degree in law, carefully explains to her son and daughter, through the pages of that book, all the facets of the problem.

One thing that Carson says, in particular, leaves young Al breathless: "Like the constant dripping of water that in turn wears away the hardest stone, this birth-to-death contact with dangerous chemicals may in the end prove disastrous."

> "Like the constant dripping of water that in turn wears away the hardest stone, this birth-to-death contact with dangerous chemicals may in the end prove disastrous."

Until then, it had never occurred to Al that progress, with all its new convenience and comfort, could also have negative repercussions. To make the message clearer, his mother offers the example of the bald eagle, the species that is both a symbol of the United States and has been endangered for fifteen years precisely because of the huge quantities of pesticides it ingests along with all the insects it consumes.

"But, Mom, if these substances really are so bad for nature and for human beings, why do they keep using them?"

"Well, Al, the situation is more complicated than it seems. During the Second World War, the chemical industry used new formulations against the insects that cause malaria. After the war, use of those same substances at home and in agriculture, as pesticides and insecticides, became widespread. And now that we know about their possible negative consequences on humans and nature, people still go on making them, because they don't want to lose money."

> ## "Are people really willing to poison themselves to make money?"

The two spend another solid half hour talking it over, but Al is left with many doubts. He has a hard time digesting everything he's hearing.

"Are people really willing to poison themselves to make money?" he asks, in a rush. "You always say everyone has rights: women, men, children, and the earth. If something is right, why do people do the opposite?"

"Sometimes the things people do make no sense. Still, you and your sister need to make an effort to see reality for what it is, however inconvenient that may be. And most of all, you need to take responsibility for your choices. The earth ought to be defended; it's your home, and the inhabitants should be protected. Now, don't lose any sleep over it: we'll just do like Old Peg, taking one step at a time, we'll get where we're going. Right?"

Just the sound of Old Peg's name brings a smile to Al's face. His father, Albert Sr., tells him the story of Old Peg every chance he gets, to remind him that, with will-power, you can attain even unimaginable goals.

With willpower, you can attain even unimaginable goals.

Old Peg was a street musician who had only one leg. Nevertheless, he was able to travel the length and breadth of America, riding a swaybacked old nag, all skin and bones, and playing a violin. With a smile on his face and the image of Old Peg in his eyes, Al falls asleep.

"Tomorrow, summer vacation is over and we're going back to Washington, so enjoy the countryside and say good-bye to the neighbors," his father tells him the next day, before Al sets out for a bike race with his friends.

He rides fast. What he's now learning, and his parents' expectations, make him want to run away. Racing through the fields of his beloved Tennessee always fills him with peace.

"Last one to the river is a chicken!" Al shouts, leaping onto his rattletrap bicycle and tearing down the slope in front of his house at top speed. He pedals faster and faster, his knees pumping high, practically grazing the handlebars. Every so often, he turns around to see how far behind his friends are.

Suddenly, he sees a cluster of frightened hens in front of him and then: "I'm flyyyyyyying!"

A moment of silence. *Safe!* he says to himself as he opens his eyes deep in a pile of hay. The shoes he sees right in front of his nose are very familiar. They belong to his father. Albert Sr. doesn't say a word. He just looks at Al Jr. for a long time. Finally, he issues an order: "Al, get home, on the double, and get cleaned up! But first go and apologize for all this mess. The hens are still trembling in fear . . ."

In fact, his father has taught him everything about the countryside.

As they walk home, Al and his father have one of their little chats.

"I love these fields," the boy says. "And it was you who made me love them and, sometimes, hate them, if you want to know the truth."

In fact, his father has taught him everything about the countryside: how to work the land with your hands and with tools, how to get water out of a well, but most important of all, how to recognize the first signs of a rut

I'll be just like him

carved out by the rain in a tilled field and how you need to disperse that water before it can carry away the seeds.

"And next year, you're going to learn to take care of our Black Angus cattle," Albert Sr. tells him. Then he turns serious and adds: "I also want you to see the work I do as a senator in the U.S. Congress, because I believe a career in politics might be right for you. You can choose to stay in the countryside, but there are people who were born to pursue just causes for everyone. You're one of those people. The world lies ahead of you, and you can make it a better place."

Al listens to him rapt: the idea of being able to change the world fills him with pride. In silence, they return to the farm. Al deeply respects his father, for his honesty but also for his strength: he is a genuine "self-made man," a person who started from nothing but built a significant, impressive career, and he has even been elected to the Senate.

I'll be just like him, Al proudly tells himself as he soaks in the bathtub to make himself presentable for dinner.

It's their last evening in the countryside that summer—a succession of fields, canoes, and animals. The next day, the family goes back to Washington DC, where they live on the eighth floor of a hotel overlooking an enormous parking structure.

In the city, Al often spends the afternoon in his father's office. On those occasions, they talk and talk, because Al has an insatiable thirst for knowledge about difficult and important subjects.

In 1965, he starts college at Harvard, where he meets Roger Revelle, the first scientist to suggest measuring atmospheric CO_2, one of the gases that causes the greenhouse effect. For many years, Revelle gathered data from the peak of Mauna Loa, the tallest volcanic mountain in Hawaii, and he went on to prove that the burning of fossil fuels is increasing the quantity of CO_2 in the atmosphere to worrisome levels.

While Al is at college, the Vietnam War begins. Once he completes his college education, in 1969, he enlists as an army journalist, even though his father's prominent position would easily have gotten him out of the draft. Before leaving for Vietnam, though, he marries his fiancée, Tipper.

When the United States loses the war, Al returns home sad and confused. To recover from the terrible experience, he returns with Tipper to his beloved Tennessee, because walking in the fields and listening to the river still has the power to make him feel all right. He grows to love its beauty a little more every day.

In the meantime, his father, in part because of his firm opposition both to the Vietnam War and to racism against African Americans, has failed to win reelection. Al is disappointed. It's not acceptable to lose if you're fighting for the right things. *Politics just isn't for me*, he decides.

He works as a journalist and dedicates himself to his new family. Al and Tipper have four children. They spend lots of time outdoors, going on long camping trips and adventuresome rafting journeys down the river.

After a few years, his passion for politics makes itself

> "The ground water of thirty-two American states is contaminated by seventy-four different chemical products for agricultural use, one of which is potentially carcinogenic."

felt again. Al commits to defending the rights of people and the earth, the way his parents taught him to do. In 1977, he's elected to the U.S. Congress as a representative from Tennessee. He organizes the first congressional hearings on climate change and invites Professor Revelle to talk about global warming. Though the data speak loud and clear, the politicians remain indifferent to the problem.

He's reelected three times to the House of Representatives, and in 1984 he's elected to the Senate. At the same time, new and worrisome facts surface. In 1988, the EPA, the U.S. Environmental Protection Agency, states that "the ground water of thirty-two American states is contaminated by seventy-four different chemical products for agricultural use, one of which is potentially carcinogenic."

Rachel Carson was prophetic!

But even this information fails to prompt any serious reactions from the governors of the various states. Al is shocked. It isn't particularly difficult to understand that when it rains, the contaminated water flows into the drinking water supplies.

He wants to be someone who makes a real difference, and he starts to dream of becoming president of the United States. And so, that same year, he runs for the Democratic presidential nomination, but he loses.

In 1989, something happens that changes his life forever: his youngest son is hit by a car while running across the street. It takes the boy a year to recover. Al gives up everything to be by his side, and he learns what matters

Al becomes the forty-fifth vice president of the United States, during the presidency of Bill Clinton.

most to him: his family and defending the earth. For the future of his children, the planet must remain livable. He gathers his thoughts concerning the importance of rescuing nature and writes *Earth in the Balance*. The book becomes a best seller. The time is ripe for incorporating environmentalism into the political agenda, and Al is more determined than ever to make a change. He brings the cause of the environment into the spotlight of an election campaign for the first time. In 1992, at age forty-four, Al becomes the forty-fifth vice president of the United States, during the presidency of Bill Clinton. Thanks to his new position, he feels sure he can devote himself to preserving the earth. Now he will be able to take up *Silent Spring* again and follow up on Rachel Carson's demands, producing real results this time.

During their two terms in office, Bill Clinton and Al Gore make serious changes: they set more rigorous standards to establish whether a pesticide is harmful to animals and humans; they reduce the use of antiparasitic chemicals; and most important of all, they encourage the use of alternative organic substances. What's more, in 1997 they lead the United States to sign the Kyoto Protocol, a global treaty designed to reduce carbon dioxide emissions and the gases that cause the greenhouse effect.

After Bill Clinton's two terms in office, Al wins the Democratic candidacy, but he is defeated by the Republican candidate, George W. Bush, in the 2000 presidential

AL GORE

election. Bush systematically dismantles all the work done by Clinton and Gore and withdraws the United States from the Kyoto Protocol.

Beaten but by no means ready to quit, Al devotes him-

> The melting of ice in the Antarctic and Greenland will lead to sea level rises of roughly six meters.

self to the defense of the environment from outside government, because, as he never tires of repeating, "Inconvenient truths do not go away just because they are not seen. Indeed, when they are not responded to, their significance doesn't diminish; it grows."

This period is marked by lectures and appearances throughout the country, with Al talking about the dangers and causes of climate change. In 2006, he writes a second best seller, *An Inconvenient Truth*, which is made into a documentary, and he founds the Climate Reality Project.

In the film, Al debunks the false scientific theories touted by global warming deniers, who minimize the terrible consequences of climate change. He proves his argument by pointing out the current state of glaciers that were once immense, such as the one on Mount Kilimanjaro (now almost entirely gone); explains that

You'll get where you're going by taking one step at a time.

the melting of ice in the Antarctic and Greenland will lead to sea level rises of roughly six meters; and goes on to warn that millions of homes are at risk of being submerged. Al is certain that the planet can be saved only through global cooperation, and he urges his audiences to act, suggesting a series of everyday actions such as recycling, planting trees, walking and cycling whenever possible, electing politicians who care about the planet, and if there aren't any running, then becoming candidates themselves.

In 2007, in recognition of his work explaining and popularizing awareness of climate change, Al receives the Nobel Peace Prize, an award he shares with the UN's Intergovernmental Panel on Climate Change (IPCC).

"So, I want to end as I began, with a vision of two futures—each a palpable possibility—and with a prayer that we will see with vivid clarity the necessity of choosing between those two futures, and the urgency of making the right choice now. . . . We have everything we need to get started, save perhaps political will, but political will is a renewable resource," Al proclaims, urging his audience, again, to vote for those who are on the planet's side.

Al Gore

Still today, Al never tires of criticizing the politicians who willfully ignore the problems threatening earth. The previous American president, Donald Trump, who withdrew the United States from the Paris Climate Agreement. In spite of seemingly insurmountable difficulties, Al continues to be optimistic, because civilization has all the necessary tools to change course. The important thing is not to ignore the truth, just as you can't ignore a stream of water running through a farm in Tennessee. You'll get where you're going by taking one step at a time, just like Old Peg!

THE LITTLE STORY OF

ADRIANA SANTANOCITO

The garden with the golden fruit

A driana carefully puts on her white-and-blue school uniform. Inside the pinafore, she practically disappears—she's very small, and everything is big on her. Her parents are worried: she doesn't seem to grow. But she's healthy as a horse, always beaming and cheerful. She loves to use scraps of cloth and other materials to make clothing for her dolls. She enjoys sketching, reading, and studying. Because she is quite brilliant, she has been allowed to skip first grade and start second grade at the Institute of the Holy Family, an elementary school in Catania run by the Ursuline sisters. She is the smallest girl in school, in size and age.

This morning, the teacher, Sister Elisabetta, is late. She arrives out of breath and sets down on her desk two bags bulging with some unknown contents.

"Good morning, children. What is this?" she asks, pulling something out of one of the bags.

"It's an orange!" says little Adriana, raising her hand.

"And that's not all! It's also a gift for Hera and her bridegroom," the teacher replies.

"Who's Hera?" Adriana asks, perplexed.

"Long, long ago, the goddess Hera was wedded to Zeus, the father of both gods and men."

"Long, long ago, the goddess Hera was wedded to Zeus, the father of both gods and men, who lived on Mount Olympus, in Greece. As a wedding gift, the happy couple received several trees that bore golden fruit. They planted the trees in a luxuriant garden, on an island in the western sea that was guarded by a dragon and nymphs. These beautiful maidens, whose song was irresistible, were known as the Hesperides. The daughters of Atlas, so unattainable and precious, filled every corner of the earth. As is so often the case with forbidden fruit, everyone wanted to eat of it. So, a king sent Heracles, a demigod that the ancient Romans called Hercules, to find the nymphs. First of all, Heracles turned Greece upside down in search of them. Then he went on to Egypt and the rest of Africa. Overcoming a thousand obstacles, he discovered that no one but Atlas, the Titan who bore the sky on his shoulders, knew where

ADRIANA SANTANOCITO

that garden could be found. Heracles hastened to the Titan's presence.

"Heracles, sitting comfortably in front of Atlas, said with great cunning, 'How weary you must be, holding up the sky all day, every day. I'd take your place, for a while, if I didn't have to gather three pieces of golden fruit for my king . . .' Atlas could hardly believe someone was willing to trade places with him.

"'I'll pluck that fruit for you,' the Titan replied, greatly content. Because Atlas was the father of the nymphs, it was a simple matter for him. Once he securely placed the celestial vault on Heracles's powerful shoulders, he ran off, light-footed. Then, at an exceedingly slow pace, enjoying every moment of freedom from the weight of the sky, he went back to Heracles. After all these adventures, the golden fruit from the garden of the gods came down to earth. Its botanical name still bears a trace of the old legend: citrus fruits, in fact, belong to the category of the hesperidia," Sister Elisabetta concludes, as she starts to hand out an orange to each girl for the midday snack.

"Teacher, does that mean the island of the golden fruit is Sicily? We're *full* of oranges!" Adriana asks curiously when the teacher walks past.

"It might be so. Our island is as verdant and luxuriant as the garden of the gods, but human beings are neglecting it. Instead, they should love it and protect it."

"*I* certainly will!" the little girl concludes resolutely. And instead of going out to play, she sketches gods and goddesses with sumptuous attire in a garden full of citrus trees.

For days, Adriana is bewitched by oranges, as if she were seeing them for the first time. She peels them and allows her hands to be suffused with their pungent scent. She touches the tip of her tongue to the rind, tasting it; then she cuts it, lets it dry. She slices the flesh and observes it closely. Then she draws the juicy little follicles that make up the carpels, thousands of drops of fruit, lined up compactly, side by side. And deep in her heart, she feels capable of heroic exploits, just like Heracles.

The years pass quickly, between summers at the sea-

> And deep in her heart, she feels capable of heroic exploits, just like Heracles.

side in Brucoli with her grandparents and her studies in Catania in the shadow of the volcano—or, actually, of the "volcaness," because Etna, to the Sicilians, is a woman. And Adriana herself seems like a volcano of creativity. Passionately interested in clothing, she dreams of becoming a designer, inventing something that will make her Sicily beloved around the world, but also cared for more sincerely by its own inhabitants. This is in the 1990s, and sadly, the garden of the gods is suffering. Garbage is dumped all over urban and rural areas; a drought is torturing the farms, orchards, and plantations; and the sea and rivers are often carelessly and indifferently polluted.

Once Adriana finishes high school, she enrolls in university with a major in business, but the siren song of fashion is stronger. After a year, though she knows it makes her parents sad, she decides to make a change in her life. One evening at dinner, she tosses the grenade:

"Mamma, Papà, I want to go to Milan to study fashion," she announces, upsetting the peace and quiet of her family's home. Her parents' reaction is resolutely negative. Then and there, Adriana accepts their refusal, but in her heart, she's still determined to carry it off on her own. For a year she designs and stitches dresses and other clothing of all sorts, selling her creations to her girlfriends and finally managing to set aside a little pile of cash. She then finds an inexpensive academy in Milan, AFOL Moda, and a place to live. At that point, she presents her dream to her parents again, who finally agree to support her, because she has a plan to accomplish it.

In 2011, she moves to Milan and stays with Manfredi, a Sicilian friend of hers, who lives with his girlfriend, Enrica, who is also from Catania. Enrica studies communications and international relations. At first, Adriana was supposed to stay with them for only a week, long enough to find a place to live permanently, but in the end, this becomes her new home. Adriana is happy. She really likes the city, even if she does miss the scents and colors of her island, those pink-and-purple sunsets that make the sea look like liquid mercury.

She concentrates on her studies and quickly passes her exams. The academy is a strong stimulus to her creativity. She's increasingly intrigued by materials and fabrics, especially experimenting with natural dyes. When she gets home, she immerses strips of cloth in a pot of boiling water, mixing in, alternatingly, coffee, tea, strawberries, and of course, orange peel. Then she fixes the color by leaving the cloth in the bathtub with water and coarse salt. Enrica has a little dog named Couscous—nicknamed Cousky—that she tends to keep locked in her room because she's afraid it might poison itself with those weird brews and compounds. In the meantime, Adriana's commitment is rewarded: she wins two scholarships, so she can continue her studies at the university without burdening her parents.

There is talk of ecology and sustainability in fashion in those years. The most farsighted researchers undertake experimentation in order to produce nonpolluting textile fibers based on organic waste, such as crab shells or corn. Adriana is increasingly convinced that this is the path she must follow. One afternoon, she attends a conference led by Eco-Age, an agency that helps the most innovative fashion houses become more eco-compatible. The founder, Livia Firth, says, "Do you know what makes fashion designers as happy as children in a playroom? A new material."

A lightbulb switches on in Adriana's head. *I'll find a new fabric*, she tells herself. Then she hurries to share what she's learned with Enrica, who has become a close friend.

"Like I did when I was a girl, I still want to invent something to put Sicily in the spotlight," she confides to Enrica over an aperitif.

Her friend turns serious and shows her a picture from Facebook. "Sicily is already infamous . . . Look at this shameful waste." It's a picture of a friend's orange grove; you can see the fruit rotting on the trees.

"Why haven't they harvested them yet?!" Adriana exclaims in astonishment.

"They're not going to, because the cost of harvesting them would be greater than any potential earnings. Oranges would need to be sold at a fair price, enough to cover the cost of production, harvest, and transport. Since that isn't the case in Italy, often those who own

> "Like I did when I was a girl,
> I still want to invent something
> to put Sicily in the spotlight."

75

citrus groves prefer to leave the fruit on the trees, rather than invest effort and money. And then there's the question of disposing of the pressed orange pulp and rinds, the *pastazzo*," Enrica explains.

Once the oranges have been pressed, the companies have to dispose of towering mountains of waste, equal to 60 percent of the weight of the fruit. In Italy, in just five months, from November to April, oranges generate seven hundred thousand metric tons of waste. The earth can't absorb such a vast quantity of garbage, and as it rots, it also taints the water table.

"But they produce oranges in Brazil, Mexico, the U.S.A., and India, as well as other European countries, such as Spain . . . Can you even imagine what a massive stream of pollution and waste?" Enrica concludes.

Adriana listens with extreme interest, and as she listens, a crazy idea takes shape in her mind. At that point, she retreats to her room and starts doing research. She discovers that some researchers convert orange *pastazzo* into flour, biogas, food for pigs, and essential oils. But these are always tiny quantities recovered at exorbitant costs. *We'd need some way of reusing the waste material on a large scale, making the production of oranges more sustainable,* Adriana thinks.

She is reminded of when she studied for an exam and learned that fabrics such as viscose and acetate are obtained from wood cellulose through a chemical process, and that cellulose can be found in all plants. *Then it must be present in oranges, too, and maybe a fabric can be obtained from that cellulose,* she tells herself, increasingly excited. This idea makes her leap to her feet. She shoots off an email to a professor of textile technologies, Manuela Rubertelli, suggesting this topic as the focus of her third-year thesis. The professor says that she's interested, but she's not going to decide right away. She'll let her know.

Adriana goes back to Catania for the winter holidays. On Christmas Eve, the city is full of light. The stalls lining Via Etnea, the main street that runs from the port up to the volcano, sell torrone nougat and glazed almonds and hazelnuts. There is the scent of sugar in the air, and the sun is warm, much warmer than in Milan. Adriana sits at a café's outdoor table and enjoys the relaxed atmosphere. She tears off the *tuppo*, the little button atop the brioche that's served with Italian ice, or *granita*. A shiny, soft little ball of dough, it reminds her of the nose of a clown, and before she bites into it, she inhales the sweet scent of its yellow crumb. When she returns home, she finds she has received an email from Professor Rubertelli. It's wonderful news: she has accepted Adriana's thesis proposal. "Get in touch with my colleague Elena Vismara, a professor of chemistry at the Milan Polytechnic. She's assigned you a laboratory to use and a female graduate student to assist you.

Talk soon." Adriana is very excited. She couldn't have dreamed of a better Christmas present.

Upon her return to Milan, she works on making a thread from the waste matter of the "golden fruit." She shuts herself up in the laboratory for eight months, taking copious and detailed notes on the progress made. It's summer 2012, and one evening, after exhausting but thrilling days, she writes, "The process seems to be working. If overnight the orange cellulose produces a film, that means it really is possible to obtain a filament. Then we can produce a new fabric. I'll call it Orange Fiber. Now I can only wait."

The graduate student who has been working along-

"Now I definitely need
the strength of Heracles!"

side Adriana opens the laboratory the next morning, as she does every day. She checks the chemical preparation and calls Adriana immediately:

"Victory! Your cellulose made a film! Are you ready to patent your discovery?"

Adriana lets out a yell and hugs Cousky, the only one who happens to be home at the moment. "Now I definitely need the strength of Heracles!" she tells the little dog, planting a kiss on his snout. From that moment on, a frantic race begins as they chase after the money to buy the Italian patent.

"You could participate in start-up competitions," the professors in the department suggest, "but to do that, you'd need a team of collaborators."

So, Adriana asks Enrica to help her. Her friend is a trusted ally and an expert in communications; she also speaks perfect English. Together they win a number of competitions. In 2013, the new fiber is patented in Italy. Word spreads rapidly in Milan, and the first fashion house to ask Adriana for a sample of the new fabric is Ferragamo. One problem: the fabric doesn't exist yet. Adriana thinks about her parents, the trust they've placed in her, and realizes the time has come to take a very big step: start a company. In 2014, with Enrica at her side, she founds Orange Fiber. Their first offices are in their apartment in Milan, and they work tirelessly. That same year, the patent is extended to the rest of the world. They need more money to produce the first thread, and that's when things get complicated: before they are willing to support the idea, the potential investors demand to see something concrete, but in order to create something concrete, Adriana and Enrica need money from the investors.

The young women's tenacity is finally rewarded: Adriana's visionary idea inspires the first three investors, who soon become her partners. Meanwhile, Adriana

Adriana feels her heart overflowing with joy. Now that the thread exists, her creativity will lead her forward.

and Enrica win prizes and competitions that fund the production of the thread prototype. They present it at the 2014 Expo Gate event in Milan, on the occasion of Vogue Fashion's Night Out. The pilot plant for the extraction of cellulose from citrus fruit is set up in Sicily in December 2015. Then, another production site is established, in Rovereto, in northern Italy. It's now possible to create the first yards of fabric. That same year, Orange Fiber is invited as the Sicilian representative of the Italian Pavilion at the international Milan Expo 2015. In 2017, the first collaboration with the Ferragamo fashion house, a "capsule collection" composed of twill, organic silk, and the golden fruit thread, is presented on Earth Day.

Adriana feels her heart overflowing with joy. Now that the thread exists, her creativity will lead her forward. Combining the filament made from *pastazzo*, which is originally white and unscented, with other fibers, she creates jersey and poplin, too. The Orange Fiber company collects a considerable quantity of citrus waste, helping to limit the pollution of the Sicilian soil and its water table, and it even purifies and reuses residual liquids after processing. The current production of cellulose is two and a half metric tons, but thanks to a fruitful crowdfunding effort, Orange Fiber will gradually increase its production facilities, with a goal of sixty metric tons of cellulose annually.

Adriana's satisfaction really is complete now. Over the years, she realizes that she has created a circular economy between citrus producers, pressers, and fashion creators—not only reducing the waste and discards in the production of the golden fruit, but also involving companies from various sectors, bringing prosperity and work to the community in addition to continual respect for the environment. Most important, she discovers that the ecological benefits of producing her fabric exceed all her expectations at the start of her adventure.

"Comparing the production of our poplin to pure cotton evidences a sharp reduction in the use of water and pesticides," Adriana proudly says at the press conference. "What's more, Orange Fiber thread does not require planting an orchard, unlike cotton. Orange trees already exist for the production of the fruit, and every year, the groves will yield new fruit, whereas cotton production entails planting new seeds every year,

"Comparing the production of our poplin to pure cotton evidences a sharp reduction in the use of water and pesticides."

occupying food crop farmland . . . You can't eat cotton, after all!" Adriana concludes with a smile.

That tiny girl used her creativity and strength, the strength of Heracles, to keep her promise to Sister Elisabetta, and every day, she takes care of the garden that bears golden fruit.

THE LITTLE STORY OF
TIZIANO GUARDINI

Long live
the caterpillar!

Tiziano is eleven years old, and every morning in the summer, his mother takes him to the camp at Villa Pamphili, a vast old park in Rome. The minute he walks through the gates, he finds female camp counselors waiting for him. While the peace and quiet of all that greenery envelops him, Tiziano stretches out on the lawn and waits for his fellow day-campers to arrive. Gazing down at the blades of grass, he observes the life teeming around him, tiny creatures hurrying along the ground: busy ants that, one after the other, in long lines, carry breadcrumbs on their shoulders; a grasshopper leaping, only to vanish who knows where; and a cricket chirping since the night before.

Tiziano is at ease. He feels that every creature is equally important.

Tiziano is at ease. He feels that every creature is equally important.

He remains motionless to keep from frightening the insects, and he breathes gently to keep from chasing away a bumblebee that is diving into a clover flower. At a certain point, he has the impression he's being watched. His eyes come to rest on a green caterpillar lying on a large daisy. It really looks as if the caterpillar were staring at him. With the lightest imaginable touch, Tiziano brushes it with his finger. The caterpillar curls up into a ring and remains motionless. At that point, Tiziano moves his hand away and sits there, contemplating it. It is a magnificent creature, alive and pulsating just like him and every other living being in that luxuriant park. He can just glimpse the caterpillar's eyes, tiny dark patches, and a strip of lighter green that runs from one end of the tapered body to the other. That afternoon, in his free time, he takes out the sketch pad he always carries in his backpack and does a quick drawing of the caterpillar.

That evening, when he returns home, he's covered in dirt, and his white T-shirt, which had been immaculate that morning, is a maze of green grass stains. Tiziano sinks into a nice hot bath. *Where have all the ants and grasshoppers that were running and leaping around me this morning gone?* he wonders. *And the caterpillar?*

After dinner, he gets out his sketch pad. The green strip that runs down the caterpillar's belly continues to slither around in Tiziano's head. He decides that that stripe would look great on a broad-shouldered jacket. No sooner said than done: he starts sketching it out. Then he combines a pair of wide-leg palazzo pants, bright yellow, with the jacket. When everything strikes him as perfect, he lightly sketches in a few more silhouettes of leaves on the jacket's lapels. He falls asleep for a moment with the pencil still in his hand. When his mother calls him, he forces himself to brush his teeth and climb into bed, but only because he knows that he's going back to the park in the morning.

"This afternoon, we're going over to see Nonna Bruna," his mother announces at breakfast. "Are you happy about that?"

Tiziano is overjoyed. His grandmother is an expert at crocheting, and at her house, there's a whole roomful of embroidery thread and balls of cotton yarn. You can find every shade or hue there, and they all go beautifully together, because Nonna Bruna has a gift for making everything match and harmonize.

"Do you want to try?" Tiziano's grandmother asks him, as he raptly observes every movement of her crochet hook and her hands.

"I would love to, Nonna!" Tiziano responds, and he immediately finds a ball of dark-blue yarn and a bottle-green crochet hook in his hands. The lessons continue, conducted by his grandmother with lots of love and patience. Tiziano does his best, but he just can't seem to produce lace that meets his own expectations. Nonna Bruna's work leaves her hands like so many flowers, full and regularly shaped, while his own creations are always a little uneven and off-kilter.

> "It takes determination and lots of practice. Keep practicing, and you'll see that you can do whatever you set out to do."

"It takes determination and lots of practice. Keep practicing, and you'll see that you can do whatever you set out to do," his grandmother reassures him. Tiziano throws himself into her arms and takes a deep breath, inhaling her wonderful smell, a mixture of hairspray and coffee. He knows that his grandmother isn't talking just about crocheting: she knows of Tiziano's talent for designing clothing, and she wants him to cultivate it.

Just after Tiziano begins middle school, his parents break up, and the years turn dark. Now that Nonna Bruna is no longer around, his sole remaining comfort is designing garments. All the same, once he finishes middle school, he follows his parents' advice—his father is a computer programmer, and his mother is an accountant—and enrolls in business school to become an accountant. As soon as he has a free minute, however, he holes up in his room, puts the music on at full volume, and designs his own fashion brand: the spring/summer collection and the fall/winter collection; skirts, trousers, and jackets. All of it sealed with signature details that allude to flowers and plants.

Tiziano continues his studies, enrolling in business school. He finishes university with plans never to open his sketchbooks again, but he realizes that a life devoted to numbers and accounting isn't right for him. And so, at age twenty-seven, without saying a word to anyone, he takes the entrance exam for the Koefia International Academy of High Fashion and passes with flying colors. For four years, he plunges into his studies as a fashion designer, venting his creativity and training to craft patterns and garments with the highest level of precision, but also learning the use of materials, the importance of finishing touches, and everything else that a fashion designer needs to know.

At dinner with his mother, he chats about his future profession, now that he's finished at the academy: "Seeing that you're a vegan and you love animals so much, what will you do when you have to work with silk?" she asks him, sipping her espresso. "I've read that in

Tiziano thinks about the silkworm problem all night long.

order to get the silk thread, they kill the silkworms by tossing them alive into boiling water or a freezer."

To make a cocoon, the silkworm produces a thread that can stretch as long as a mile. Inside that cocoon, in perfect safety, the silkworm is transformed into a butterfly. Then, in order to leave the cocoon, it cuts the thread, which thus becomes unusable for traditional weaving methods.

"I've thought about that a lot, actually. I'm going to find an alternative. And if there isn't one, I'll create it myself," he replies resolutely.

Tiziano thinks about the silkworm problem all night long. He knows that as a fashion designer, he's going to have to deal with all types of fabrics, but the sheer idea of causing so much death upsets him.

"I'm never going to use silk if it means killing all those silkworms. They're living creatures. Can there really be no other solution?" he confides the following morning to a friend.

"A method was invented in India years ago. It's called ahimsa silk—that is, "nonviolent silk"—which is made by joining the ends of the threads cut by the butterfly without having to kill any silkworms," she replies.

"They treat silk threads like the short fibers of linen and cotton, spinning them together to make a single long thread?" he asks excitedly.

Tiziano flies to India to see how this pain-free silk is produced and processed. This is the beginning of "Three Days to Butterfly," his first ahimsa silk collection. Before long, Tiziano also discovers soy silk, which costs a bit more than traditional silk, but also offers considerable advantages: it's very strong, is nonallergenic, and it won't catch fire. With this fabric, he creates the "Soya Silk" collection, fifteen one-of-a-kind items with graphic motifs of bees, butterflies, winged rhinoceroses, dragonflies, and millipedes.

> The older Tiziano grows, the less he can tolerate the infliction of suffering on animals.

The older Tiziano grows, the less he can tolerate the infliction of suffering on animals. He's increasingly determined to reject any and all compromises, especially after experimenting with cruelty-free fabrics and materials. In 2015, he learns that the feathers used for down and for decorations are plucked brutally from geese, rather than being harvested in periods of the year when the animals shed them naturally. For his clothing,

Tiziano replaces goose down and feathers with pampas grass blooms—sand-colored tufts that create an equally soft and fluffy effect.

His creations are featured on the covers of international fashion magazines. They're one-of-a-kind items, so impregnated with nature that they almost become part of it.

One summer evening, as he lies under the leafy branches of the trees, breathing in the muggy air, Tiziano

His creations are featured on the covers of international fashion magazines. They're one-of-a-kind items, so impregnated with nature that they almost become part of it.

realizes how intertwined humans and plants really are.

He then gathers a great many fallen branches, strips off and breaks apart the bark, stitches the flakes into a fabric, and constructs a dress that turns anyone who wears it into an almost magical creature, half woman, half tree. Thrilled by the result, he goes back to the park, gathers more materials, and creates a pine needle fur coat, another clothing sculpture that can be worn like any ordinary jacket, complete with a zipper. Then, again turning to trees, he creates a tube dress made of pine cone scales in his father's garage/workshop.

"Do we have to pierce them each, one at a time?" his father asks dubiously.

"Yes, Papà," Tiziano answers with a smile. "Thanks for your help. It's been such a long time since we did anything like this together." The two men make a perfect team: the father pierces the pine cone scales with a fine-point drill bit, and Tiziano strings them on a thin thread, creating a fabric unlike anything that's ever been seen before. That evening, when the tube dress is ready, they go back to the park, leaving the remains of the pine cones where they first gathered them. And the circle remains unbroken.

In no time at all, these nature-inspired garments are seen around the world, put on display in prestigious museums in London, Vietnam, the United States, and even at the United Nations.

In September 2017, Tiziano participates in the Green Carpet Challenge, a competition for young fashion designers distinguished for their use of ecological and sustainable materials. The winner's outfits will be worn by Hollywood stars to promote respect for the planet. Tiziano wins the competition with a vivid blue dress made of soy silk and decorated with beads made from old CDs and empty mussel shells. Worn over it is a long jacket made out of plastic gathered from the Mediterranean Sea and fishing nets from the seas off Korea. A genuine triumph, it launches Tiziano to the highest reaches of high fashion. Newspapers and magazines from all over the world hail him as the "fashion designer of nature," the creative who honors the sacredness of life with the beauty of his garments.

Tiziano does not intend to rest on his laurels, though. He knows that there is always more that can be done to restore the planet's health. And so, he starts searching for alternatives to leather, a material that, in both its production and disposal, is a massive pollutant that causes the death of many animals. He discovers that there is a kind of imitation leather that uses discarded fruit. He's truly happy, and he resolves to work with that material. It is, however, still strictly experimental.

The opportunity arrives a few months later. At a conference on textile innovation, he meets a group of researchers who excitedly tell him about their discoveries concerning grapes. With dried grape pomace, they can create a paste that, when spread in multiple layers, becomes a soft and sweet-smelling textile entirely similar to leather.

Tiziano signs on enthusiastically and gives life to the world's first "Wine Leather" collection, which consists of handbags, shoes, and suits of a decidedly vermilion hue.

One afternoon, while organizing his closet, he finds an old pair of jeans. He is a big fan of denim, and he wishes he could use it in his suits. But he's also well aware of the harmful nature of denim production. The chemicals and dyes poison the workers and pollute the environment around the factories producing it. There must be an alternative to this, too, he decides. He starts digging into the matter and, this time, discovers that the solution is recycling. One of the world's biggest jeans manufacturers produces denim from recycled cotton and polyester—that is, from used PET-type plastic bottles—without polluting. And so, Tiziano starts designing articles in denim, thus making a new ecological, highly fashionable product.

Tiziano is often asked to speak about his experience, both because he has become an international symbol of sustainability and because, thanks in part to the example he has set, many fashion designers are converting to sustainable fashion. At the end of 2019, in order to prove that sustainable fashion does not require renouncing beauty, Tiziano presents most of his new discoveries in a runway show. First, he transforms the room into a luxuriant forest, filling it with panels of ecological denim treated with Airlite, a special, nonpolluting colorant that purifies the air of bacteria, smoke, and mold.

Then he creates garments that, in their every fiber, speak of his love and respect for nature: his socks are made of organic cotton; the denim in his jeans is ecological; the yarn and threads used in his suits and dresses are made of discarded fishing nets; and his down jackets

95

are filled with a material made from plastic bottles, carpets, and upcycled wool.

"To make the world of fashion a more ethical and just place, what we need above all is determination," he says at the end of the runway show, inwardly recalling Nonna Bruna's encouraging words.

"Today, sustainability involves various aspects of manufacturing, from reuse of water to photovoltaic solar power installations on the roofs of companies; from the selection of fabrics and materials to the reuse of everything that already exists. Fashion must be mindful of the future, nature, and all living creatures," he sums up, satisfied.

The following morning, Tiziano is at Villa Pamphili. He lies on his belly on a soft lawn, the way he used to as a little boy. He observes the teeming life beneath him, moving silently between blades of grass. He takes a deep breath, inhaling the sweet smell of moist, living earth. Then he turns onto his back, puts both hands under his head, and watches the clouds race past overhead. Tiziano is happy now—he knows that he is doing all he can to respect life, even in its smallest forms. He smiles as he thinks back to the caterpillar on the daisies from his childhood. "You see? We've done it. We've found grace and beauty in clothing without harming anyone," he says to the caterpillar with a wink of his eye.

THE LITTLE STORY OF
WANGARI MAATHAI

You can't stop a river

Wangari's dark eyes fear nothing.

"You are a Kikuyu, and your name is Wangari, like the leopard," her mother tells her as she sends her out to get firewood. "They're just like you. There's no need for you to be afraid."

Wangari isn't afraid of anything. In her little Western-style white cotton dress, she prances agilely into the forest of the Aberdare Range without making a sound.

Gathering wood as she goes, she reaches the banks of the Kanungu River, which in that section of its length is still just a narrow strip of water. She sets down the branches she's gathered and climbs up to the source of the river, a tiny hole in the ground from which spurts a

"You are a Kikuyu, and your name is Wangari, like the leopard," her mother tells her as she sends her out to get firewood. "They're just like you. There's no need for you to be afraid."

99

spring of cool, incredibly clean water. It seems impossible that this could become the great river that runs downstream. She lowers her head and drinks eagerly until her thirst is slaked, careful not to step on the frog's eggs that, like so many tiny colorful beads, cluster under the high leaves of the prayer plants.

There's still time, she thinks. I just have to get back before sunset.

There's still time, she thinks. *I just have to get back before sunset.* She shuts her eyes and takes a deep breath of the humid air. Then she walks along the banks of the little river until she reaches the foot of a *mugumo*, the wild fig tree with bark the color of an elephant's skin. At this point, she removes her sandals in a sign of respect, as is customary among the Kikuyu, then lets herself sink to the ground. She lies there, motionless, watching as the sky and the branches spin around her. For the Kikuyu—one of the many ethnic groups in Kenya—the *mugumo* is a *murema-kiriti*, which means "one who resists the cutting down of the forest." In fact, you're allowed to cut one down only when another has been planted next to it, to ensure that its spirit can find a new home.

Full of energy now, she goes back to carefully selecting the driest and most seasoned firewood, to ensure it doesn't produce smoke. The sunset bird is already singing its melody, and Wangari realizes that she's running late. Soon, darkness catches her by surprise, filling the sky with stars. She's tempted to linger a bit—not even the night scares her—but she doesn't want to frighten her mother. So, she takes one last glance at the Milky Way and hurries back to the family's mud hut. Her mother is standing in the doorway, waiting to dine with her beneath the starry sky.

"Soon you'll go to school," she tells Wangari, who is just eating her last bite of cooked green bananas.

The food almost gets stuck in her throat. "Go to school? Me, too? Really?" she asks in disbelief.

"Why not? You're curious, and you're a fast learner," her mother concludes with a smile.

Wangari is only six years old, but she is already catching a whiff of a new life. Not everyone in Kenya goes to school, girls even less than boys.

While her family is busy preparing her for school, the United Kingdom, which still rules Kenya at the time, is carrying out a major deforestation enterprise. In place of the *mugumo*, they have planted pine and eucalyptus trees, which grow fast and can fetch good prices for the lumber industry and for construction.

And so, the forest changes, many animals disappear, and groundwater—which had previously been preserved by the mighty roots of age-old trees—grows scarce.

WANGARI MAATHAI

Wangari doesn't notice the changes because she gets up so early in the morning to get to school, and walks for miles along a new road, far from the forest—also, because nothing distracts her from her studies. In just a few weeks she's the top student in her class: she learns the alphabet, mathematics, Swahili, English, and geography. Then she returns home, like all Kikuyu girls, and helps her mother with household chores.

One day, she learns a lesson that will prove useful for the rest of her life. At dawn, she sets off with the family's donkey to gather red beans on the family's plot of land, a few miles from their home, on the other side of the hill. Once she reaches the vegetable patch, Wangari carefully chooses each bean pod, filling one sack to the brim and another halfway. At sunset, she puts the full sack on the donkey's back and hoists the half-full one onto her own back. The return home is challenging because both she and the donkey cannot bear the weight. Wangari doesn't complain or spill a single bean. She wants to do her work well, and the last thing she wants is to cause her mother concern. Suddenly, the donkey slips, and Wangari teeters. Will she be able to lift an animal and its burden all by herself? she wonders. Then she pushes, pulls, and drags the donkey until it rises to its feet with the sack on its back. They reach home late at night and collapse to the ground, exhausted.

"I probably gathered too many beans," Wangari tells her mother, "but I've learned that willpower can lift mountains. And I have plenty of it."

WANGARI MAATHAI

"I probably gathered too many beans," Wangari tells her mother, "but I've learned that willpower can lift mountains. And I have plenty of it."

Wangari is a very determined little girl, both at home and at school; there isn't a challenge she can't overcome. In 1951, after finishing elementary school, she's admitted with the highest possible score to St. Cecilia's Intermediate Primary School, on the slopes of Mount Kenya. There the students wake up at dawn, say their prayers before going to Mass, and then take baths and brush their teeth; only then does the school day start. At this boarding school, no one is allowed to speak Kikuyu—only English—and if any of the girls reverts to her native language, she must wear a badge of shame. At first, these rules are difficult to accept, and Wangari feels a bit confused. In her mind, however, she can always hear her mother's words: "You're between two worlds, just like a tree. Go confidently toward your future, fill your branches with new fruit and flowers, but never forget where your roots lie."

All things considered, Wangari likes life at the boarding school, and most of all, she loves to study—and she's brilliant at it. At the end of the term, she passes her exams with flying colors, and she's admitted to the only high school for girls in Kenya. There she meets a person who is destined to change her life: Mother Teresia, the science teacher who will help her become the tree her mother talks about.

"Will you help me wash the glass slides and test tubes?" the teacher asks her when class is over.

Wangari, who is fascinated by microscopes and other laboratory instruments, is in seventh heaven.

> It makes her feel that nature has its own equilibrium, just like that day in the forest of Aberdare, along the Kanungu River.

Little by little, biology, with its study of life forms and the laws that govern them, captivates her entirely: it makes her feel that nature has its own equilibrium, just like that day in the forest of Aberdare, along the Kanungu River.

In 1959, at the age of nineteen, Wangari graduates. These are times of astounding new developments for Kenya. The years of English colonial rule are ending, and freedom is in the air. The Kenyans have voted for

WANGARI MAATHAI

the first time, and now what is needed is a new African governing class, made up of honest individuals ready to rule and lead. Wangari has great dreams for her future and for Africa's. One year later, she's one of the three hundred best students in Kenya, and she wins a scholarship to study at Mount St. Scholastica College in Atchison, Kansas, where she will spend the next four years. After getting her undergraduate degree in science, she is chosen to pursue her master's degree in biological science at the University of Pittsburgh, in Pennsylvania.

She returns to Kenya in 1971 to assist a professor of zoology in Nairobi, but she suffers a gross injustice. The position for which she was specially summoned back to Africa from the United States has been assigned to a man who belongs to the same ethnic group as the professor. Even though Wangari is right, she is roundly ignored. She understands that Kenya, now free of English rule, has to reckon with a new set of problems: women don't have the same rights as men, and corruption is rampant.

Everyone who has ever achieved what they set out to do has been knocked to the ground repeatedly, Wangari tells herself. *They get up, dust themselves off, and keep trying.*

Everyone who has ever achieved
what they set out to do has
been knocked to the ground repeatedly.

And that's what I'll always try to do, just like that day I carried the red beans with the donkey.

In fact, a few years later, she becomes the first woman in the country to get her doctorate, and she is appointed director of the Kenya Red Cross.

In 1974, she is invited to join the local committee of Environment Liaison Centre International, an independent organization established to enable citizens to collaborate with the United Nations as environmental activists. In order to provide a report on the situation in Kenya, Wangari needs to understand what is happening in her country. First, she goes back to the countryside where she grew up, at the foot of Mount Kenya, and there she sees the effects of climate change. In the summer, it practically becomes a desert. When it rains, the rivers swell immediately, and the hills collapse in landslides. What's more, the cows that were once well fed now wander aimlessly, undernourished, in search of the increasingly rare blades of green grass.

Her mother greets her, clearly concerned. "After planting the eucalyptus trees, they established tea and coffee plantations everywhere for the international market, even taking over the village vegetable patches. The

The big sacred trees are all gone now, and there isn't enough water anymore.

big sacred trees are all gone now, and there isn't enough water anymore," she tells her daughter.

"Our children are no longer strong and healthy as they used to be. Now they eat only the industrial food we buy, because we no longer have the vegetable patches we once had, nor firewood to cook with," say the local women who have come to greet Wangari: they are clearly very worried.

Wangari is aghast. When she was a girl, no one suf-

And so, in 1977, during World Environment Day, the women plant together the first seven trees in a park just outside Nairobi.

fered from malnutrition, and the earth, green and rich in water sources, was sufficient to feed everyone. She understands that poverty and the exploitation of the environment are two sides of the same coin.

"You know lots of things; you've studied a great deal. What can we do?" the women ask her desperately.

"Let's plant trees. They will give us firewood to cook with as well as storing the water in their root systems so that the rivers finally form again. And if we plant fruit trees too, they will give us food to eat."

Wangari invites the women to go into the remaining forests to gather local seeds, so that they can replant trees suitable to their land. And so, in 1977, during World Environment Day, the women plant together the first seven trees in a park just outside Nairobi. This is the beginning of a women's political campaign that will come to be known as the Green Belt Movement.

"That's what it's called, because together we can create a belt of trees around the desert regions and our vil-

> "We will fight the desertification that results from the mistreatment of the earth."

lages," Wangari announces proudly.

As they plant a tree, each participant utters a solemn commitment:

"We will fight the desertification that results from the mistreatment of the earth. Deforestation brings drought, malnutrition, hunger, and death, and we commit ourselves to preventing any action that can deprive future generations of the resources that belong to us all."

In a very short time, the Green Belt grows into a nongovernmental organization based in Nairobi. In 1985, during the Third UN World Conference on Women, in Nairobi, representatives from various countries around the world witness how many new fruit trees and trees for firewood were planted and are already growing.

They honor Wangari's tireless efforts and undaunted courage by establishing the Pan African Green Belt Network, an international collaboration among fifteen countries to combat desertification. Working together, the member countries will create a greenbelt of nearly thirty million trees the length of sub-Saharan Africa.

But planting trees also means planting ideas, and the growth of the Green Belt Movement soon runs up against the corruption of the government, its vested interests, and its violence. Wangari receives numerous threats, but she doesn't retreat, because the cause she is defending is a just one.

In 1989, the President of Kenya wants to build an illegal sixty-story skyscraper in the only green area in Nairobi, Uhuru Park, to make it the headquarters of his

> Wangari receives numerous threats, but she doesn't retreat, because the cause she is defending is a just one.

political party. Wangari and the activists of the Green Belt Movement oppose the project, writing letters to the newspapers and to the authorities of countries all over the world.

"Will the big park that provides the city with clean air and peace really be destroyed?" they all ask vigorously, denouncing the government's secret plans.

In response, Wangari is jailed and accused of posing a danger to the state. The scandal spreads far and wide, and many international organizations rush to her defense. Even the U.S. vice president, Al Gore, demands she be set free, and he threatens to suspend U.S. foreign aid to Kenya. In the end, Wangari is released.

But the corrupt government continues to exploit the parks for its own vested interests and to give away land to friends and supporters. In 1998, the next target is the

However, the activists return to the park in ever-greater numbers, and finally bring the government workers over to their side.

beautiful Karura Forest nature preserve, an urban forest at the confluence of four rivers, where age-old trees and protected animals are now being threatened by teams of workers sent by the government.

Once again, Wangari and the Green Belt Movement inform the citizenry. The female activists are threatened by the workers sent by the government; the men carry *pangas*, short machetes. However, the activists return to the park in ever-greater numbers, and finally bring the government workers over to their side. The deforestation is slowed, but before the situation can change entirely, they'll have to wait for the inauguration of the new government, in 2002.

Wangari is appointed assistant minister at the Ministry for Environment and Natural Resources by the newly elected government. In 2004, all her efforts are recognized, and she becomes the first African woman to win the Nobel Peace Prize.

"We are called to assist the earth to heal her wounds and, in the process, heal our own," she says in her Nobel Lecture. "Through the Green Belt Movement, thou-

"Together we are that river."

sands of ordinary citizens were mobilized and empowered to take action and effect change. They learned to overcome fear and a sense of helplessness and moved to defend democratic rights."

Though Wangari is no longer alive, the Green Belt Movement continues to thrive. In the last forty years, the organization has planted more than 51 million trees, and more than thirty thousand peasant women have been employed to carry on Wangari's message:

WANGARI MAATHAI

"A great river always has a source. Often, it's tiny, as is the case with the Kanungu, where I used to gather firewood as a girl, but when it encounters other tributaries, it becomes so big that nothing can ever hope to stop it. Together we are that river."

THE LITTLE STORY OF
RIGOBERTA MENCHÚ TUM

The highlands are my home

L ittle Rigoberta, five years old, is pushing her way laboriously through the branches of the big trees that surround her leaf hut. She belongs to the K'iche' ethnic group, an ancient indigenous group descended directly from the Maya. Ever since her father and mother used their life savings to obtain authorization to cut down trees to build their leaf hut, they have lived in the tiny *aldea,* or village, of Laj Chimel, on the slopes of the mountains of Guatemala, where they cultivate milpas, or corn crops, their chief source of nutrition.

Rigoberta dearly loves her homeland, with the sky almost always a dazzling blue and the stream that sings loudly with the birds.

Rigoberta dearly loves her homeland, with the sky almost always a dazzling blue and the stream that sings loudly with the birds—even if she has to walk for hours and hours to reach the closest neighboring village, and even if it's often so hot that she can't breathe or so cold that it makes her teeth chatter.

Before the corn ripens, the whole family travels down-hill to work at the *finca*, the landowners' plantation, where they stay for at least seven months.

"Hurry up, Rigoberta, the truck won't wait for you!" her father shouts, and the little one hurries, grudgingly, to clamber aboard. Packed in with the animals, she hates the two-day, nonstop journey.

"Papa, when are we going to stop harvesting coffee?" she asks when she can't tolerate the motion sickness any longer.

"When we have enough food on our mountains."

"And when will that be?"

"When the corn grows, when our chickens give us eggs and our sheep give us milk. Then we'll live hap-pily on the highlands."

Rigoberta feels encouraged, but then she remem-bers the last flock of sheep that vanished into the forest because there hadn't been anyone to watch over them, and the nausea surges up inside her again.

The plantation is on the coast. Grown-ups and chil-dren are hard at work harvesting coffee. The harvesters sleep together, lying on the ground, and often the families are separated for months on end: mothers and children over here, fathers and elder brothers over there.

Rigoberta is very familiar with the powerful connection linking humans and animals. She understands that harming animals can only hurt humans, and vice versa.

Where is my nahual *now? What is it doing? It must be free and happy in the mountains*, the little girl thinks with a sigh when she can't get to sleep at the *finca*. In Mayan mythology, a *nahual* is a personal guardian spirit that manifests itself in the form of an animal. Everyone has their own *nahual*. It is determined by your day of birth according to the sacred calendar, and it is concealed from all other people.

Rigoberta is very familiar with the powerful connection linking humans and animals. She understands that harming animals can only hurt humans, and vice versa.

She is a good girl who does no harm to anyone and who does her best to help her parents.

At the plantation, she works hard and never complains, as if she were already a grown-up.

When they harvest the coffee, the field hands have to take care not to snap the branches of the plants. Otherwise, the landowners will dock their pay. If they're not careful, they may wind up working a full day for nothing.

"You were too slow," the landowners scold her.

"You broke some branches," they lie.

"We'll deduct that cost from your wages," they tell her, then turn to leave.

She feels an overwhelming impulse to break down, but her empty stomach ties itself in knots, and she holds back her tears, as if trying to fill it. The same thing happened when her little brother died, and no one on the plantation could do a thing to help him. The *patrones*, the Spanish owners of the plantation, hadn't been around for days, and her mother, who had no more money, had been unable to buy medicine or even feed the little boy.

When the family finally travels back to their mountain region, where the corn is now high and full grown, Rigoberta is happy. As they climb to Laj Chimel, not even the winding road bothers her.

Life up there is exciting, even if it's exhausting too. You're free up there, you breathe sweet-smelling air, and you're all together, your community, which is just like an extension of your family. Often it rains heavily, and

> Life up there is exciting, even if it's exhausting too. You're free up there, you breathe sweet-smelling air.

Rigoberta, who has only one set of clothes, dries them in the sun and the wind, without a word of complaint. What matters to her is to be accompanied by her siblings, and to see that her father and mother are well. At age nine, she starts to work with a hoe in the fields alongside her father. She follows him all day long and learns what she can.

She plants beans, sets up little sticks when the seedlings sprout, protects the corn from the weeds, and harvests osiers, which she then sells at the market to make wicker baskets or furniture.

Before long, just like her brothers, she is using a machete, a large knife people here employ to split firewood and cut their way through the forest.

Thanks to the edible herbs of the fields and the corn, which they use to make delicious tortillas, Rigoberta and her family manage to stay in the highlands for months without having to go down to the *finca*. The land up there is fertile, and just like their ancestors, they grow beans, squash, and chili peppers to sell at the market.

Turning twelve is an important landmark in the community. This age marks the beginning of adulthood and the end of being a dependent within the family. That day, Rigoberta gets up early and braids her hair with special care. At breakfast, her father gives her a sweet little piglet. "Her life is in your hands now. You will be responsible for raising this pig, and you'll have to do it

RIGOBERTA MENCHÚ TUM

alone," he tells her proudly. Her father is not only the most remarkable person Rigoberta has ever met, but he's also the spokesman for the community.

Rigoberta feels honored by the new task assigned to her. "I'll take care of her," she promises, lifting the piglet high in the air and then hugging her tight to her chest.

That day, in celebration, they roast a chicken in the village. It hadn't happened in years because Rigoberta and her people eat meat only on really special occasions.

The pig is a female. She grows fat and happy, and when the time comes, she gives birth to five piglets. Rigoberta is expected to feed them without relying on the family. And so, in the evening, once she's done with all her other work, the little girl starts weaving. In order to see at night, she sets fire to the *ocote*, the wood of the Montezuma pine, and weaves the cloth that she will sell at the market. With what she earns, she buys bran for her swine. In order to continue feeding them, she grows more corn in a patch of farmland her father has set aside for her.

"I'm really proud of you," he tells her one evening. "Your piglet has given birth to a litter of healthy little ones. You have a good relationship with animals. That's a gift from your *nahual*."

"You're a native, just like me!" Rigoberta says to one of the piglets, and it leaps into her arms and stares into her eyes, as if it wants to ask her something. "And that is a word I like—*native*—because it means that we were both born here, in the land of our ancestors. We don't exploit the earth and the people the way the *patrones* do. This is our home, and it always will be."

> My voice will join the larger voice of the village, because all together, we'll pray, we'll work, and we'll share our food.

Then she looks up and turns her eyes to the highlands. "You wound the earth only when it's absolutely necessary," her father had explained to her. That evening, with the moonlight illuminating the river and the fields, she understands better than ever what he meant by that phrase.

Tomorrow, she tells herself, I too will follow the ritual of our ancestors. I'll ask the earth permission to plant corn by tilling the soil more gently. My voice will join the larger voice of the village, because all together, we'll pray, we'll work, and we'll share our food.

As she grows up, Rigoberta decides to become a catechism teacher. She was taught Christianity as a girl by the priests of Catholic Action, who come up to the village every three months. "God" is like a good father who lives in heaven. He does not conflict with her own tradition, which teaches to venerate nature's elements. What's more, Rigoberta loves the stories of the Bible because they resemble those of her own ancestors. Unfortunately, she cannot read as much as she would like; nor can she communicate with most of the priests, who speak only Spanish. She knows only the language of her community, K'iche', one of more than twenty different languages spoken in Guatemala. At the *finca*, too, it pains her not to understand what the *patrones* say. She especially hates not being able to respond appropriately when her masters try to cheat someone, stealing their hard-earned money. Injustice makes her angry right down to the tip of her braid, which is very long.

And so—to help her parents, but also to learn Spanish—as soon as she can, she goes to the city to work as a housekeeper. Life in the homes of the *patrones* is even harsher and crueler than on the *finca*. They give her lots of orders and very little food.

"I'm going to dock you the next two months' salary because I had to buy you a pair of shoes. You can't walk around our house barefoot. You'll get the floor dirty," the mistress snarls. Rigoberta puts up with it all. She can't wait to get back to the highlands with the small pile of cash she's managed to save over the past months, but her satisfaction is shattered by a piece of terrible news.

"Papa is in prison," she learns from her brother, who has just arrived in the city.

"What on earth for?" Rigoberta asks.

"Because he tried to defend our lands from the big landowners who were determined to take them away from us."

"But those lands have been ours forever! Plus, the inhabitants of the village have paid taxes to stay there since long before we were even born."

"The problem is that no one else can understand our language. We need to pay an interpreter who can translate into Spanish what our father is saying."

So, off she goes, to find an interpreter. But the landowners beat her to it, and they bribe the interpreter. Rigoberta's father is in trouble again. The interpreter assures him that the land will remain the property of the indigenous people for all time. The document her father signs, however, states that it is theirs "only for two years." After a period of peace and quiet in the highlands, one terrible day, the *patrones* reappear.

"This land belongs to us now. You signed the paper," they scold him, waving a sheet of paper that no one understands, as trucks and earthmovers push their way through the trees.

The situation is deadly serious. The community gathers and asks Rigoberta's father what to do.

"We must remain united, fight side by side," he replies. Remaining united is really the only thing they can do, because the *patrones* immediately occupy the houses, empty the pantries, and force them out. The villagers become homeless under the scorching sun and driving rain. Even armed soldiers arrive. This is guerrilla warfare, and the community organizes as best it can. Rigoberta, who knows how to win an audience, draws up escape plans and defense maps for the indigenous people. Others stand sentinel and announce when the military arrives. While the women and children distract the *patrones*, the wanted men run away into the forest, where no soldier dares venture. The most courageous young men take on the soldiers with machetes or by throwing rocks and tossing chili powder.

Rigoberta's father is shuttled in and out of prison. As soon as he can, he comes back to the community to tell them the news—none of it good—from the city.

"They won't leave us be. They'll come back. But even if they've assigned us lands far apart from each other to separate us, we'll rebuild all our houses close together! Together we will resist, together we will be strong," he says, and in the meantime, with the most determined farmers, he founds the CUC, the Committee for Peasant Unity.

In the meantime, the tireless Rigoberta travels for hours through the mountains, from one village to another. She learns that indigenous people everywhere are being forced off their lands, which are being confiscated by the army, and she encourages them not to give up the fight.

Hundreds of indigenous people, including her father, mother, and a brother are killed in what, by now, amounts to a full-blown civil war. Rigoberta takes her father's place in the CUC and carries on his struggle. She has realized that, in order to be able to unite, it is necessary for the *indios* to be able to understand each other. By day, she works hard at the *finca,* and by night, in total secrecy, she learns as many indigenous languages as possible, so that she can continue to organize the resistance movement in the villages. Thousands more peasants join the protest movement, and factory workers and many Christians fight alongside them, supported by priests and nuns. The government reacts by sending tanks to attack the crowds and bombing the villages from above. There seems to be no limit to the atrocities. Rigoberta is wanted by the police. Sometimes she is afraid and weeps for her parents, but then she bolsters her courage and tells herself:

"I'm not the only orphan in Guatemala, and I must never stop fighting to ensure that no native is ever again left without land or starves to death."

In 1992, Rigoberta is awarded the Nobel Peace Prize "in recognition of her work for social justice and ethno-cultural reconciliation based on respect for the rights of indigenous peoples."

RIGOBERTA MENCHÚ TUM

Her voice travels a long, long way, and the tragedy of the *indios* horrifies the worldwide public.

In 1992, Rigoberta is awarded the Nobel Peace Prize "in recognition of her work for social justice and ethno-cultural reconciliation based on respect for the rights of indigenous peoples."

"I consider this prize," says Rigoberta, in Norway, where she accepts the award, "not as a reward for me personally, but rather as one of the greatest conquests in the struggle for peace, for human rights, and for the rights of the indigenous people, who, for five hundred years, have been split, fragmented, as well as the victims of genocides, repression and discrimination." Then she pauses, thinking back to her village, her neighbors and relatives who were killed, and her life on the highlands, and goes on to say:

"I call upon all the social and ethnic sectors that constitute the people of Guatemala to participate actively in the efforts to find a peaceful solution to the armed conflict."

"I call upon all the social and ethnic sectors that constitute the people of Guatemala to participate actively in the efforts to find a peaceful solution to the armed conflict."

Since that day, Rigoberta has never stopped telling the world that defending the earth also means giving dignity and peace to those who live on it:

"We need to focus on an ecological development that can ensure the survival of populations and safeguard the balance of nature, which lies at the root of our culture, which is in turn the patrimony of humanity at large."

In part as a result of her words, four years later, peace returns to Guatemala.

RIGOBERTA MENCHÚ TUM

THE LITTLE STORY OF

PIERRE RABHI

Like a hummingbird

Little Pierre unrolls the mat on the roof of his ochre-hued house in the Algerian oasis of Kénadsa. The still-warm tiles comfort his back as the early crescent moon sets and the sky is filled with stars. His nose turned up, he remains motionless, gazing at the heavens, and when a falling star shoots past, a twinge of fear clamps his throat shut. *It's the angel Gabriel, riding into war against the Djinns, the evil spirits,* he thinks. Hearing his father playing the lute downstairs reassures him. His father is a tall, strong man. Ever since Pierre's mother died, he's done all he can to comfort Pierre and be close to him. He's a blacksmith, but he's also a poet and a sage, and everyone in the village respects him. To the sound of his music, Pierre falls asleep like a grain of sand lulled by a cool breeze.

When Pierre smells the scent of pepper and cinnamon rise from the ground floor, he knows it's time to go to school. His aunt helps him get into his white outfit, runs a hand through his hair to tidy it, and walks him to the door. "Don't forget your dates," she tells him, putting four sweet, fleshy fruits in his hand.

Pierre immediately bites into one and then races off toward school. He prances barefoot from one shadow to another to keep from scorching the soles of his feet. "You're a little gazelle!" his grandmother tells him one day, and then she proceeds to tell him one of the scary stories he likes so much.

Pierre has recently begun Koranic school and learned how to prepare the clay writing tablet—in the oasis where he lives, they don't use sheets of paper—and trace the first letters of the Arabic alphabet.

After school, Pierre stops to admire the minaret. The white tower of the mosque, which rises tall and imposing above the village, looks out at the mystery beyond the wall of stone and sand that protects the oasis. The first place Pierre goes is his father's workshop. He wants to learn to heat iron and spray sparks in all directions by pounding the iron with a hammer on the anvil. "The world is changing. You need to go to school," his father tells him instead. And so, the "little gazelle" returns home by taking the quickest route, which allows him to stop and play in the garden of a fellah, a farmer. He loves the cool freshness of the damp soil, but he especially enjoys lingering to chat with the owner, who works in the large vegetable patch directly behind Pierre's home.

"Why is your field green while elsewhere everything is yellow?" Pierre asks him one evening.

"Because the shade of the palm trees refreshes the earth, allowing the lower plants to flourish. In turn, those lower plants capture and hold the water from the spring in their roots, and release a little every day. The water moistens the soil and transforms the seeds into the vegetables you eat. That is the miracle of the earth!"

That night, lying on the roof, Pierre awaits the angel Gabriel while thinking about the palm trees, the water, and the miracle of the earth.

> "Why is your field green while elsewhere everything is yellow?"

But everything is about to change.

The French colonists who run the administration of the territories discover coal deposits near the oasis, and they hire miners to extract it. In a short while, the pace of life in the community is upended by the quickening pace of work. Pierre's father shuts down his forge to become a miner. Every night, he comes home black with coal dust and increasingly sad. When he walks through the door, he sighs loudly. Afraid that Pierre might be forced to work as a coal miner, too, he sends him off to be raised by a French family in Oran, in northern Algeria.

Early one morning, he calls to Pierre and tells him, "Here is your new mother." Pierre gulps, opens his hazel eyes wide, and scrutinizes the face of a woman with light-colored hair who smiles at him kindly. Certainly, he misses his mother—he still feels an immense hole in his heart—but this lady with skin the color of milk is so sweet smelling and kind that the little gazelle lets her hug him.

When the time comes to leave for his new home, Pierre holds tight to his father's strong, gnarled fingers, but already his new life awaits him and is full of absurd things. The French family eats in strict silence, at a table, not hunched over on the floor on a ram skin. They don't emit a belch at the end of the meal to express that the food was delicious. His new mother and father are *roumis*, or Christians, and they don't pray five times a day. What's more, their apartment is on the sixth floor—high enough to make your head spin!— with straight, cold walls and lots of furniture and other objects filling the rooms. They sleep on high beds in their own bedrooms, not side by side on mats laid on the floor. Where are the aromas of pomegranates and figs? Where are the colors of the desert at sunset? Where the stars of the oasis? And their clothing is a pain: suits with suspenders, instead of robes! Pierre likes walking barefoot and feeling the warm earth under his feet, but now: "No. Put on your sandals!"

Pierre feels like a fragile tree in a tempest. What a disaster: a little gazelle that can no longer run!

Slowly, he rediscovers his peace of mind. After all, now he has two families, two cultures, two languages to explore. He's also learned to read in French. And in Oran, he even sees his first cars go roaring past, and trains, which look like extremely long snakes. Plus, there's the sea!

A few years pass, and Pierre finishes his new studies. Then he starts a job in an office. He likes his new position; it makes him feel grown-up and free. But early one morning, while the city is still sleeping, he sees something strange from his balcony: thousands of French soldiers, a great bustle of military vehicles and people shouting, "It's war! Algeria is at war!"

Before they close the ports, Pierre decides to try his luck in France. So, he boards an enormous ship, and after many days of sailing, he reaches Paris.

The metropolis is immense. All the streets are brightly lit, people crowd the squares, and cars and trolleys flow by without stopping. Everything seems magical, and yet there's something about it that saddens him: he can go a whole day without a single person saying a word to him. Yet the city is full of posters with smiling faces that invite him to come on in, buy, see, and visit!

But all alone? At the oasis, there was always someone willing to offer you a cup of tea and a pleasant chat.

Pierre finds a position as a specialized worker in a big factory. The work is simple enough, but soon the unhappiness becomes overwhelming. He misses light, nature, and life in the open air. He feels as if he's been imprisoned, like a mouse in a box. The factory is a box full of people who work and say nothing to one another. The room he lives in is small, also like a box. The trolley is a long box full of people packed in together, and the cafés are boxes full of sad people.

Can you really live your whole life trapped in a box? he wonders.

In the spring, he meets Michèle, a petite secretary with large green eyes and hair in tight black ringlets. He falls in love with her immediately. There they sit, under a tree, talking about how wonderful it would be to be free and live far from the city! Together they seek a place where they can live off the land and raise animals. Their friends think their plans are sheer madness, but Pierre and Michèle refuse to give up. They continue to search, read, and contact everyone they know. One day, a friend tells Pierre to write to Dr. Richard, an extraordinary man who created the Vanoise National Park and who is now trying to create the Cévennes National Park, in southern France.

"Dear Pierre and Michèle," Dr. Richard replies to their letter. "In our region there are old abandoned farms you could buy and then devote yourselves to cultivating. But since the land is poor and rocky here, it won't be easy. If you're strong and brave, and you have a little money, this is the place for you! Together we can bring these beautiful lands back to life."

Pierre hugs Michèle close to him, and together they start to dance for joy: they're about to head south.

They travel the whole way hand in hand, in silence, their rapt gazes absorbed in the landscapes streaming past the window. They're heading toward their future.

What now?

"Point one," says Pierre "is to find a place to live!"

"But, no. Before point one, point zero: learn how to be a farmer! Pierre, you need to study," Michèle says. "You can't just make farming up as you go along." And Pierre knows that she's right.

In the low, bare building of the school of agriculture, Pierre is the oldest student.

Can you really live your whole life trapped in a box? He wonders.

"Only by cultivating crops with modern methods, using chemical pesticides and heavy machinery, will we be able to defeat world hunger," the teacher says over and over again.

Pierre takes notes, even if he disagrees. He knows that back home, life was just fine before the advent of moder-

While the soil in the fellah's vegetable patch was dark and soft, and the vegetables grew in lush abundance, even if it was in the middle of the desert!

nity. By "just fine," he means tranquil, making do without needless things, with only as much as was needed to eat, live together, and be happy. So, he listens in silence and does his best to learn everything, but in his mind, he's already making a list of things he will never implement, determined as he is not to harm nature.

Pierre has gotten a good look at the soil in these areas: it's dry, impoverished by chemicals, exploited relentlessly. The soil is like a tired old horse that can no longer run—while the soil in the fellah's vegetable patch was dark and soft, and the vegetables grew in lush abundance, even if it was in the middle of the desert!

After three years of study and practical experience, Pierre becomes an agricultural laborer, or farmworker, and he can now request a loan to buy a farm. Pierre works hard, day in and day out. In the meantime,

PIERRE RABHI

Michèle works as a secretary in a small city not far away, to put aside some savings.

They spend weekends together, roaming from one valley to another, exploring forests, rocky gorges, and roads that are a succession of curves, in search of a farm to buy. One fine day, after driving through a dense forest full of maple trees—lo and behold, they see a simple stone house placed dead center on a high, wind-swept plateau. All around are chestnut trees and lots of sandy, arid land. Pierre's heart lurches momentarily: that land, so brown and faintly hostile, reminds him of his oasis. But—in fact, there's more than one *but*—there's no electric power, and there's no drinking water. There will be plenty of work to do, and it's going to take time, courage, and dreams. The two young people join hands, shut their eyes, and imagine themselves living happily with their children and their nanny goats.

The next day, they go to the bank and apply for a loan, and before they know it, they're committed. The neighbors are happy to have a young couple living nearby: as Pierre discovers, even in the mountains, you can be lonely.

Pierre starts tilling the soil. In order to make the land fertile again, it's going to take months of hard work and lots and lots of manure, which Pierre procures by cleaning the shepherds' stalls and stables. One day, a neighbor brings him a packet of seeds that have been widely advertised on television: "Miraculous seeds that produce bell peppers the size of pumpkins!" Pierre plants them, and sure enough, the bell peppers grow to an enormous size, but they're virtually flavorless. What's more, after the second harvest, the plants seem to go on strike: they don't produce any more peppers. How can that be? Pierre goes down into the cellar and gathers a handful of the seeds from his own small and irregularly shaped bell peppers, homely but delicious. From that day forth, he reminds himself: good seeds, just like good fertilizer, are fundamental.

One evening, as the sun is setting, Pierre stops to

Lost in his reckoning of infinite possibility, he smiles as he realizes that by respecting nature, he can find food for one and all.

admire his wheat, which has finally grown after months of failed attempts. He plucks a stalk of wheat and thinks, *With this we could nourish all mankind. Every stalk of wheat has forty kernels, and each kernel could create a new stalk! One hundred stalks of wheat are four hundred kernels. This is a miracle of the earth!*

Lost in his reckoning of infinite possibility, he smiles as he realizes that by respecting nature, he can find food for one and all.

Pierre tries out a variety of farming techniques, but one in particular catches his fancy: it's called biodynamics, a system that uses only organic fertilizers. And there, by the light of the moon, his hazel eyes look right into Michèle's large green ones.

"Are you ready?" he asks her.

"Yes," she replies, as serious as a priestess in ancient times. Together they pile up a mound of dirt and organic waste (fruit rinds, leftover vegetables, dry leaves, and twigs), adding to it compounds of yarrow, nettle, and chamomile. Then, taking careful instruction from a book by Rudolf Steiner, the inventor of biodynamics, they cover it with a tarp. The heap of dirt must be sheltered from the rain and wind. Two months later, sure enough, the magic has worked! The vegetable scraps have created a rich, dark-brown soil, soft, sweet-smelling, and teeming with microorganisms and oxygen: it's humus. This soft new earth is better than any chemical fertilizer, and soon their fields are full of delicious fruit and vegetables.

Word spreads, and more and more people come to hear Pierre lecture on the importance of agroecology, that is, the best way of living off the fruit of the earth while taking care to keep the soil alive—in fact, even better than it was before the fruit was cultivated. In just a few years, Pierre is well known throughout France. He's invited to speak to audiences of hundreds

PIERRE RABHI

of people. And he, a little man tipping the scales at just 125 pounds, shares his experience and argues that the earth belongs to everyone, but especially to "the children of the future, those who will come after us!"

He becomes renowned outside the boundaries of France. "You must go back to Africa and remind those who have forgotten the miracle of the earth," a friend tells him. "The situation in Africa right now is an utter tragedy. Where they once grew enough to feed themselves, they are now starving. The land is dead. And before you have a chance to say no, I want to tell you a legend."

"In a forest one day, a great fire breaks out, and all the animals prepare to make their escape. Only a small hummingbird travels from the river to the flames, taking a tiny drop of water in its beak each time and letting it drip onto the fire. From the safety of a rock, a large armadillo mocks the bird: 'What do you think you can do with those tiny drops of water? You can't be dreaming of putting out the fire?' 'I don't know, I'm just doing my part,' the hummingbird replies, and continues flying incessantly."

Pierre is deeply struck by the story. "If we all did our part, however small, together we could change the world," he thinks out loud. And then, at last, he replies, "I'm going to Africa."

He embarks on a great adventure that continues today. After that first trip, Pierre Rabhi is summoned to Burkina Faso to found the first African agroecology training center. A few years later, the United Nations recruits him as an international expert on food security to fight against desertification, the process by which fertile lands become desert. He returns to Africa to teach local communities how to procure food while respecting the earth and the people who cultivate it. This leads to the creation of agroecological oases in Morocco, Niger, and Mali.

In France, a community of Orthodox nuns enlists him

> "If we all did our part, however small, together we could change the world."

to revive the health of fields left sterile by years of chemical agriculture. A group of Buddhist monks ask him to help open a nature reserve, that is, a large park where a vast array of plant species and varieties are preserved. A billionaire invites him to transform his abandoned lands into orchards and vegetable patches and fertile fields. Over six hundred "Colibri" communities—named after the hummingbird—are founded, where people help each other, care for the earth, share food, and live in wonderful solitude. Thus, Pierre re-creates a great many new "oases" where everyone can live happily.

THE LITTLE STORY OF
JADAV PAYENG

My *karma bhumi* for the earth!

It's been raining for days in the village of Kokila-mukh, in the state of Assam, in the foothills of the Indian Himalayas.

"Hurry, let's get our things and run away!" Jadav's father, Lakhiram, exclaims as he comes running into the hut. "The Brahmaputra is furious. It's about to over-flow its banks again, and it will sweep the village away." Quickly and quietly, the family piles up their possessions at the center of large tarpaulins serving as suitcases: the straw mats, a few terra-cotta bowls, and a copper pot to cook in, and on top of them, a small heap of clothing. Hastily pushing their cattle, they move with the rest of the tribe to the surrounding hills.

This isn't the first time that the Mishing are forced to pull up stakes and start over from scratch elsewhere. The whole village, with all its cabins and huts, uproots itself and moves away to a new location on the map, venturing ever higher, ever inland from the shores of the island of Majuli.

As soon as they're all safe, the father assembles his children:

"Nature is sacred. She's our mother. We are Mishing, and we adapt to her will. You will have to learn this," he tells them. Then he sums up, tersely, "While I build a shelter for tonight, you little ones milk the cows and take the milk to your mother, who'll use it to make cheese for the market."

Jadav obeys, but he is lost in thought. He's four years old, and he has already moved twice. He adapts to the new situation, like everyone else in the tribe, but he can't figure out what's happening. In the evening, he sits on the straw mat next to his father and, gazing right into his eyes, whispers to him, "Maybe the Mishing people and the river aren't getting along anymore. Maybe someone made the river angry, like when mother suddenly stops talking to me. There's always a reason."

"Jadav, the river floods because of the monsoons, the winds of the rainstorms, or because of the snow melting high on the Himalayas. Nature makes decisions that humans have to accept. There is no disagreement between us and the river," Lakhiram replies. Jadav trusts his father's judgment and falls asleep.

"Nature is sacred. She's our mother. We are Mishing, and we adapt to her will. You will have to learn this."

The village slowly recovers, and ordinary life resumes. The following year, in 1969, the monsoon rains start again, a hard and driving downpour, a wall of water, as if there were no room between one drop and the next. At dawn on the third day of showers, the Mishing are awakened with a start by a powerful and low-pitched roar: it's the Brahmaputra River, which once again comes rushing through, sweeping away everything in its path. This time, even the cows are hit by the flood, and Jadav's parents are barely able to escape from their hut and carry their children to safety, dragging their feet through the water, which rises as high as their necks.

All is lost: no cattle, no milk, nothing to eat.

Once the fear subsides and they have looked all their loved ones in the eye to make sure they're all right, the two parents consult in low voices, to keep the children from overhearing.

"We've lost everything. We can't feed them all. You know that, don't you?" Lakhiram murmurs gravely.

"Jadav can go to stay with Judge Borthakur, who buys cheese from us every day. He is a good person. He always says that he wants to help us send at least one of our children to school. . . . Now we're going to have to accept his offer," Aphuli, the mother, replies, holding tight to both her husband's hands. Her eyes fill with tears.

"Jadav, come here," his father finally says, in a loud voice.

The little boy trembles slightly: he recognizes that serious tone and knows he can make no objections.

"Tomorrow we'll go to Jorhat, and you'll move in with the judge, that important gentleman who always buys from us. You'll live with him, help him, and obey him, as well as go to school," Lakhiram announces, without waiting to hear any reply.

Jadav doesn't say a word. He throws himself into his father's arms and hugs him tight. He knows that his parents would never willingly be separated from him unless it were absolutely necessary. Jadav's siblings and mother, all crying together, join the collective hug.

"It won't be forever," his father says in a gentler voice. "Just long enough to breed another herd of cattle, and then we can all live together again."

For their part, his parents work hard to rebuild their business; and Jadav studies in order to earn a better future for himself. But that's not the way things turn out.

When he's fifteen years old, Jadav's father and mother die, and he returns to the countryside to look after the family's animals: cows, water buffalo, and hens. During the trip to Kokilamukh, however, he's forced to stop a few miles from the coast, to wait for the floodwaters of the Brahmaputra to subside. After two hours on foot under a blazing sun, and a canoe trip through floating branches and the detritus from huts and cabins. he finally reaches the shores of his island.

He looks around and has difficulty getting oriented: where there was once a canal, it's all dry land; where it was difficult to make your way through an intricate tangle of branches, now there's an expanse of arid dirt without a bit of shade. He walks around a massive pile of rocks, and his eyes are dazzled by an expanse of sand unlike anything he's ever seen.

Why are there withered branches, he wonders, *if there are no trees here anymore?* He approaches, his curiosity aroused, and realizes that what had struck him from a distance as irregular lengths of wood are, instead, hundreds of dead, desiccated snakes. They were overwhelmed by the flood, just like his cows all those many years ago, and without trees to protect them from the blazing sunlight, they died. Crushed by his grief for all those poor creatures, Jadav falls to his knees and bursts into tears.

Today it happened to them, tomorrow it could be us, me and all my people, he thinks as he sobs.

He would dearly like to ask his father for advice, but

Today it happened to them, tomorrow it could be us, me and all my people.

he's all alone. And so, he thinks back to his father's words: "You're a Mishing. You need to adapt and survive." Jadav musters his strength. *Yes, Papa, I'll survive, but I can't accept all this without taking action. At school, I learned that man can even travel to the moon, so maybe I can prevent other creatures from having to die in such an atrocious fashion.*

Nature is now my family, so I must care for it, he thinks, resolutely.

That night, he tosses and turns on his mat. He decides that he'll ask for help from the men of the forest bri-

> **Nature is now my family, so I must care for it.**

gade, who manage and care for a large park near Jorhat. Early the next morning, he sets out. When he reaches the place, he heatedly recounts what he's seen on the island.

"Boy, you're nothing but a shepherd: look after your animals and forget about matters that are so much bigger than you. The forests, which hold back the floods with their roots, are shrinking everywhere, and there is nothing that can be done about it."

"That's not an answer," Jadav retorts. "You're forest rangers. Your dharma, your duty, is to care for the forests and the animals that live in them. The law of dharma says that you may fail, but you must act, try."

"So, now you're going to give us a law lesson? Maybe it's *your* dharma. Why don't *you* do it? And just let us do our own work," the eldest forest ranger concludes with annoyance and goes back to digging up a flower-bed with his hoe.

His nerves set on edge by such indifference, and determined to find a solution, Jadav stops at the village of Deuri Gaon on his way home. He intends to visit a wise man of whom his father once said, "He lives in harmony with everything."

When he comes face-to-face with the man, Jadav makes the greeting of the *anjali*, a show of respect, folding his hands together before his forehead. Then he sits down in the lotus position, legs crossed. At a gesture from the wise old man, he tells him all about the snakes, the river, and the forest rangers.

The wise old sage looks at the young man and appreciates his determination to protect the animals of the forest. Then, all at once, he stops him with a wave of his hand and asks, "Well, seeing that you want to save them, what do snakes eat?"

"Eggs!" Jadav replies promptly.

"And where do eggs come from?"

"Birds!"

"And where do birds live?"

"I understand. I must plant trees! But nothing grows in the sand . . ."

"You do understand, but you must still start from the bottom: plant the world's tallest grass, bamboo, which grows quickly, even in sandy soil."

Jadav leaves the village, his heart filled with hope and, on his back, a bagful of bamboo sprouts and seeds that the old sage has given him.

"Even though I was born a shepherd, planting trees will now become my *karma bhumi*, my daily action to be carried out on Earth's behalf. And the animals will have shade and food," he pledges to himself. For a year, every morning, before milking his cows, Jadav plants new seedlings and saplings, and slowly, gradually, a small strip of greenery starts to cover a few square yards of the island. He also brings to the spot a handful of ants, to help the plants transport their seeds from one corner of the expanse of sand to another. He realizes, however, that more sprouts are dying than surviving and taking root and that he still has a great deal to learn.

One day, fortune smiles on him: he learns that in Kartik Chapori, just a few miles from his home, they're hiring apprentices for a reforestation project covering five hundred acres. Jadav applies and is accepted immediately. Starting the very next day, he wakes up before

"Even though I was born a shepherd, planting trees will now become my karma bhumi, my daily action to be carried out on Earth's behalf."

sunrise, tends to his animals, plants a few trees in the clearing of the serpents, and by nine o'clock is ready for work as a forest ranger. In 1983, the project comes to an end, and the workers abandon the site. Jadav is nineteen years old, and he's learned everything he needs to tend trees and coax them to grow. The rangers have even explained to him why forests shrink and have confirmed what he thought when he was a little boy: that man has broken a pact of harmony with nature. In order to harvest lumber or increase the amount of land under tillage for agriculture, whole forests are being clear-cut everywhere you look. That means that the Brahmaputra no longer encounters obstacles, and when it overflows its banks, it sweeps away everything in its path, eroding the land and leaving the animals homeless and families without resources—which is exactly what happened to his tribe, over and over again.

Jadav decides that he's going to continue encouraging the forest of Kartik Chapori to grow, even if he has to do it by himself.

"This island is my land, my home, and here my children will flourish in the shade of the trees that I plant. I'll do it until the plants and trees join the forest of snakes. It will be an immense park, one where animals, trees, and people can live together happy and safe," he solemnly promises.

"This island is my land, my home, and here my children will flourish in the shade of the trees that I plant."

In the spring, he plants tamarind, mango, and mulberry trees, as well as medicinal plants. The rest of the year, he plants seedlings and harvests seeds. The inhabitants of the surrounding villages, seeing him arrive every day with seedlings and new branches to graft, start to call him *Molai*, or "Forest." Jadav is honored by that title. Above all else, he loves admiring the trees as they grow ever thicker and denser. It stirs him with special emotion that he has continued the work of the forest rangers: what was once just a sandy clearing infested with snakes is now a teeming hotbed of trees and insects.

At age thirty-nine, he meets Binita, who becomes his wife. Together they raise three children, breed cows and water buffalo, and make cheese just like Jadav's parents.

In the meantime, attracted by the shade and the shelter that the forest now offers, a great many wild animals return to live under its canopy; while others travel through the forest just to rest, refresh, and continue to the nearby Kaziranga National Park.

Jadav's efforts have brought back to the island everything: apes, birds, snakes, rhinoceroses, deer, wild boars, and elephants—and even the increasingly rare Bengal tigers.

At times, these Bengal tigers push their way into the surrounding villages, tearing livestock limb from limb. Jadav is forced to offer explanations to the local residents, urging them not to let their animals graze too close to the forest because, as we all know, "Tigers aren't interested in farming!" He himself loses over a hundred head of cattle over the years, but he never loses his temper. He's just happy that all the sowing of seeds and planting of seedlings he's done over the years, every single day, without respite, has brought life back in all its varied forms. Even the Mishing tribe has been able to recover a shred of stability, farming and living in the shade of the trees. Many of the inhabitants also help Jadav to plant new trees. At last, the Brahmaputra seems to be less out of control, thanks to the strong roots of the forest, which restrain its fury.

But the biggest problems, needless to say, are caused by the elephants. In the summer of 2008, the herd that comes to stay on the island for at least six months, in order to rest and spawn little ones, consists of at least one hundred individual specimens. Hungry and curious, the pachyderms even venture into the villages and eat most of the harvest, arousing the villagers' anger. In fact, the villagers lash out and kill several elephants. As soon as Jadav learns of what's happened, he calls the authorities, determined to find a solution and reconcile villagers and elephants.

When the forest rangers arrive, after failing to check in on the condition of the trees for twenty-five years, they are stunned. There are more than twice as many trees as on their last visit, and they now cover the entire island of Majuli. There are fourteen hundred acres of greenery, twice the size of Central Park!

Word spreads quickly, and everyone in the region wants to meet the man who single-handedly refor-ested an entire island. From that day on, Jadav receives numerous prizes and awards. In 2015, he's given the title of Padma Shri, one of the highest honors India can bestow. The Majuli forest is nicknamed "Molai" in his honor, and he is now known the world over as "the Forest Man of India." Jadav delivers many lectures at schools and universities, because, he says, "We all must learn to respect the pact between humans and nature." And he always ends every meeting and lecture with the same exhortation: "Plant trees!" Then, as he has been doing for over forty years, he enters his forest to plant a few seeds.

The Little Story of Greta Thunberg

Give us back
our future!

"Greta, turn the light off when you leave the room," her mother, Malena, tells her, taking a break from her practice as an opera singer.

"Don't we have enough money to pay the bill?" Greta replies, annoyed. They have the same exchange every day.

"No, Greta, that's not the point. I'm telling you this because we shouldn't waste electric energy. Did you know that we use nonrenewable resources to produce electricity, such as oil and coal, and that these lead to an increase in greenhouse gases?" her mother asks, setting down her sheet music.

"And what do greenhouse gases do?" Greta asks, her curiosity piqued.

"Come here," Malena says, inviting Greta to come sit next to her on the sofa. She opens a drawer in a cabinet under the window and pulls out a picture of a well-dressed gentleman with a droopy mustache.

"That's Great-Uncle Svante!" Greta exclaims with a smile. The serious chubby face has always made a good impression on her. "What does he have to do with gases?"

Her mother explains to her that at the turn of the last century, Svante Arrhenius was the first scientist to draw a connection between the increase in greenhouse emissions and the rise in Earth's temperature. Then, seeing her daughter's look of confusion, she explains: "Burning fossil fuels puts large quantities of greenhouse gases into the atmosphere. Those gases trap sunlight and thus raise the planet's temperature. This is the phenomenon of global warming."

"And what happens if the planet warms up?" Greta persists, watching those hard words stream past her eyes, determined to capture and decipher them.

At this point, Malena picks up her laptop and invites her little daughter to search for the words she doesn't know.

That afternoon marks the moment Greta, who's just six years old, starts to understand a little, but also the end of

That afternoon marks the moment Greta, who's just six years old, starts to understand a little, but also the end of peace and quiet in the Thunberg home.

peace and quiet in the Thunberg home. At every opportunity, the questions rain down. Her father, Svante, who bears the same name as her scientist ancestor, responds to most of them because he spends more time at home than Malena. In the meantime, the photo of her great-uncle enjoys pride of place in the young girl's bedroom, right above her bed—as if she believes he himself can answer her questions.

Given everything she reads, Greta, by age eight, already has a pretty clear idea of how the planet's climate is changing. When her teacher announces that the class is going to watch a documentary on the subject, she prepares to give the matter her utmost attention. Sitting in silence at her tidy desk, she cradles her face in her hands. The teacher pushes the Play button, and the documentary begins. The narrator's voice explains that there's plastic everywhere, on the land and in the water, even in the stomachs of animals that ingest it, mistaking it for food. Moreover, areas in a state of drought are spreading, and glaciers are shrinking due to the rise in temperatures. Last of all is footage of a famished, horribly skinny polar bear wandering from one ice floe to another.

"It's people, through their actions, who cause climate change," the teacher points out, and a knot forms in Greta's throat. *How can people knowingly do harm to other people?* she asks herself in anguish, as tears start to roll down her cheeks. She's deeply upset. Everything she has read now takes concrete form in the plastic suffocating fish and in the polar bears starving to death. Just as when she solves a puzzle, images form in her mind and words are joined together, and it becomes clear to Greta that everything is deeply real. Once the documentary ends, and her schoolmates go outside for recess, Greta sits motionless at her desk. She can no longer go out to play; she can no longer do anything.

At home, she sits on the sofa in silence.

She feels awful thinking about the bears, the plas-

> "It's people, through their actions, who cause climate change."

tic bobbing in the water everywhere, and the humans who are causing harm and who refuse to change their ways.

Her father has a hard time getting her to tell him what happened. Greta explains to him that she's afraid of mankind's capacity to destroy the world. Svante tries to console her, promising her that, for starters, the family will stop using plastics. And he adds:

"Don't despair. People really can change."

> "Don't despair. People really can change."

Only partly relieved, Greta dives back into climate data, numbers, and statistics. She is searching for solutions. But the more she studies, the sadder and more determined she becomes. One day, during a trip to a museum, she notices some panels containing inaccurate data on the quantity of carbon dioxide present in the atmosphere. Greta gets angry and shortens her visit. She can't stand the idea that anyone might lie or play fast and loose with the facts on anything as crucial as our planet's survival. When she gets home, she refuses to eat. Starting the next day, she declares, she will no longer attend school.

If this is a dark period for the Thunbergs, for Greta it's outright apocalyptic: thoughts of death and destruction whirl through her mind, preventing her from living like any ordinary eleven-year-old. In just two months, she loses twenty pounds, and her mouth never relaxes into a smile. Her parents tell the doctor that she hardly ever even speaks anymore, except with those she knows very well.

"It's called selective mutism," the doctor replies. "Greta chooses whom to speak with because she finds it extremely difficult to communicate. Your daughter also suffers from Asperger syndrome. She has a vision of the world completely devoid of half tones and shades of gray, which makes her extremely rigorous and demanding."

Those afflicted with Asperger syndrome tend to focus more than others on life's incongruities. They see the world without nuance: everything is either right or wrong, black or white.

The pain that Greta feels for climate change is ever-present. It's like a sentence highlighted in blazing orange on a white sheet of paper: it's something she cannot stop thinking about.

For three years, she stops going to school. She spends her time studying facts and memorizing statistics about CO_2 emissions, among other things, or perched on a

> "If climate change is real, then they shouldn't be talking about anything else on the television."

stool next to the kitchen window clipping articles out of the paper and arranging them chronologically and by subject. Then she speaks her truth to her parents in a way that almost frightens them:

"If climate change is real, then they shouldn't be talking about anything else on the television. If burning fossil fuels is so harmful that it can undermine our very existence, why isn't it outlawed? And why do we go on doing wrong things, even at home?"

The Thunbergs quickly move from trying to console her to accepting her proposals. In order to pollute less, her mother, who is a singer and travels frequently, stops taking airplanes to concerts and agrees to perform only in places she can reach by train. In the city, she starts going everywhere by bike. Greta's father buys an electric car, becomes a vegetarian like Greta, and cultivates a small vegetable patch outside the city. These actions go some way toward placating his daughter's anguish, and Greta thinks, *If my parents can do it, then other people can change, too.*

At age fourteen, Greta agrees to return to school. A year later, thanks to everything she's learned about climate change, she writes a highly detailed scientific article for a competition held by the Swedish newspaper *Svenska Dagbladet*, and her entry is declared the winner. She is immediately contacted by a local activist group, whose members are astonished at the expertise shown by such a young person. With her parents' permission, Greta meets with them. Together, they try to hold demonstrations and protest marches, but they are unable to come to any sort of agreement, and the group breaks up. But by now, the word *protest* is stamped in blazing orange type in Greta's mind.

One afternoon, Greta reads a post on the internet about a group of young Americans who refuse to attend class in protest of the arms trade.

"A strike! That's how I can get everyone to understand that, unless we mobilize, global warming will kill us all."

"A strike! That's how I can get everyone to understand that, unless we mobilize, global warming will kill us all," she announces to her parents, and then rubs her face against her dog Moses's soft coat. Now Greta knows what to do.

After breakfast on August 20, 2018, she arranges her chestnut hair into two perfect braids, the way she likes it best, puts on her favorite dark-blue sweatshirt and checkered shirt, and goes down to the garage. She prepares a wooden sign, writing on it: SKOLSTREJK FÖR KLI-MATET, which means "School Strike for the Climate." Her heart is beating fast because she's about to show everyone the fruit of years of work. She rides her bike to the Parliament and sits down on the ground, her sign perched on her knees. Greta has decided that she's going to go on strike until new elections are held.

The first day, she's all alone, and she barely receives the occasional fleeting smile. The second day, some young people stop, their curiosity aroused. On her third day in front of the government building, a small, peaceful group has started to form. Starting on the sixth day, the protest is trending on social media all over the world, due both to Greta's daily Instagram posts and to pictures taken by passersby.

Her parents are worried that Greta is missing too much school, but they can also see that she's full of life and energy again, brimming over with plans and projects, and their relief is greater than any lingering concern. In the meantime, the protest is spreading through the other cities in Sweden, and when Election Day rolls around, Greta achieves her prime objective: a discussion is held in the Swedish Parliament concerning climate change.

On September 8, 2018, the People's Climate March is held all over the world, and the organizers of the event in Stockholm invite Greta to speak about her thoughts and experiences. Svante and Malena are afraid she won't

SKOLSTREJK FÖR KLIMATET

be able to put up with the tension of being in the presence of such a huge crowd of strangers. It's still a tremendous effort for her to communicate.

"Do you feel up to it, Greta? You're not obliged to do this. You've already done so much. You're only fifteen years old," her mother tells her as she's helps her braid her hair.

"I have to do this, Mother. My little problem is nothing in comparison with what's going to happen if people can't understand that our home, the earth, is in flames. This is the time to act!" Greta replies, looking both her parents in the eye.

Her speech in Stockholm is terse, harsh, and precise. It leaves the audience breathless. They all sit listening, rapt. Greta announces that from now on, every Friday of every week, she is going to continue protesting in front of Parliament until Sweden reduces its carbon emissions to zero.

Great-Uncle Svante would be standing at my side! she thinks with a smile. This is the beginning of Fridays for Future, school strikes that spring up everywhere in the blink of an eye. Greta continues striking in Sweden, and

"This is the time to act!"

as soon as she is able, she travels across Europe by train or electric automobile, accompanied by her father, to deliver speeches and meet with the great and powerful. She is determined to push them into action.

In November of that same year, Greta is invited to give a TED Talk, a series of lectures in which experts from all over the world discuss in just a few minutes the topics they know best.

"Nor does hardly anyone ever mention that we are in the midst of the sixth mass extinction, with up to two hundred species going extinct every single day." Greta says in a firm voice in her talk.

She also talks about climate justice: "Rich countries like mine need to get down to zero emissions within six to twelve years so that people in poorer countries can heighten their standard of living by building some of the infrastructure we have already built—such as hospitals, electricity, and clean drinking water."

She sums up with these words: "And yes, we do need hope. Of course, we do. But the one thing we need more than hope is action. Once we start to act, hope is everywhere. So instead of looking for hope, look for action.

> **"We are in the midst of the sixth mass extinction, with up to two hundred species going extinct every single day."**

Then and only then, hope will come today."

In just a few months, Greta's contagious energy spreads, and soon there are almost three hundred cities hosting Friday for Future strikes.

In December, Greta is in Katowice, Poland, where, after a two-day trip in her father's electric automobile, she takes part in COP-24, the UN Climate Change Conference. There she meets with the United Nations' secretary-general, António Guterres. In late January, she moves on to Davos, Switzerland, for the World

Economic Forum, where some of the most urgent matters facing the world are under discussion—another thirty-hour trip, this time by train. Greta rattles her audience to the bones with her speech:

"I want you to panic, I want you to feel the fear I feel every day. And then I want you to act. I want you to act as you would in a crisis. I want you to act as if the house was on fire, because it is."

Greta's message even reaches Australia, where other students are starting to go on strike. The prime minister orders the kids to go back to school, threatening punishment otherwise. Greta retorts on Twitter: "Sorry,

"I want you to act
as if the house was on fire,
because it is."

prime minister, this time we can't obey."

In February 2019, Greta is in Brussels, speaking before the EU's Economic and Social Committee: "They are hopeful that the young people are going to save the world. But we are not. There is simply not enough time to wait for us to grow up and become the ones in charge."

"We know that most politicians don't want to talk to us," she says. "Good. We don't want to talk to them, either. We want them to talk to the scientists instead. Listen to them. Because we are just repeating what they are saying and have been saying for decades. We want you to follow the Paris Agreement and the IPCC reports. We don't have any other demands. Just unite behind the science—that is our demand." Then she leaves and joins the Climate March being held in the city.

Her efforts begin to yield extraordinary fruit. On March 15, 2019, in more than 2,000 cities and 124 countries all over the world, the Global Strike for the Future is held: 1.5 million students march peacefully to defend the planet; it is the largest global political march for the climate ever seen.

By now, Greta is an environmental leader: *Time* magazine names her Person of the Year for 2019, and she's a candidate for the Nobel Peace Prize.

"Global warming is an important element of social

> "There is simply not enough time to wait for us to grow up and become the ones in charge."

instability. Climate change is now one of the leading factors of poverty, famine, war, and migration," the nomination states. Greta feels honored and continues bringing her message tirelessly to the world. She goes to the Vatican and even shows one of her signs to Pope

Francis, who immediately declares his support and, with a smile, urges her to continue the work she is doing.

"I'm proud of you," her father tells her when she returns from Rome. "And your Great-Uncle Svante would be proud of you, too. You've changed our lives, and now you're an inspiration to a whole generation. You can't stop now." Greta hugs him. "I have no intention of stopping, Papa. Help me make a new sign."

THE LITTLE STORY OF
SEBASTIÃO
SALGADO

The earth saved my life

efore the sun grows too hot, Sebastião hops on his horse and takes off at a gallop. He races through the fields of tomatoes and the patches of corn until he reaches a bend in the Río Doce, where it is shady and cool. He dismounts and ties his horse to a tree. Then he takes off his T-shirt and plunges into the water. Birds with long, brightly colored plumage fly overhead, and sunshine filters down through the branches of the huge trees, strong already even though it's still morning. On the muddy river bank, a dark-green caiman slides into the water. Sebastião spots the caiman's triangular head just skimming the water's surface, but he's not afraid. He knows that the big reptile won't attack him: its favored prey are fish or small animals. He watches the caiman swim away and then plunges underwater again. Once he's refreshed, Sebastião steps out of the water and lets the breeze dry his skin.

"We're leaving tomorrow," his father reminds him as soon as Sebastião returns to the farm.

Sebastião hasn't forgotten this fact, and he's excited about the great journey awaiting them. His parents, in fact, own an enormous farm in the state of Minas Gerais—in Aimorés, to be exact, in southeastern Brazil. Thirty families employed by Sebastião's father live and work on the farm. They grow potatoes, rice, corn, tomatoes, and fruit, and they raise pigs and cattle. Once a year, they bring their livestock to be slaughtered, riding horses for more than fifty days. Sebastião is ten years old, and this is the second time he has set out on this long ride.

> Once a year, they bring their livestock to be slaughtered, riding horses for more than fifty days.

In the morning, he gets up early and helps his father round up the animals. His mother joins them with provisions. Once the other herders arrive, they all finally set out on horseback, animals in front, men behind, Every dozen miles or so, when the cattle are exhausted, the group stops and pitches camp.

"Sebastião, get under a tree immediately!" his mother orders. "The sunlight is too strong here!"

Sebastião, whose skin is very fair and burns easily, obeys and sits down under a large, leafy tree. From there he looks around at the backlit land. His mother, cooking food, is a dark silhouette surrounded by a dazzling glare; and so is his father, busy unloading the blankets from the horses' backs.

Sebastião likes that contrast: partly coal-black world and partly too-blinding white—and he's in the middle, in a halfway kingdom, commanding everything.

Sebastião likes that contrast: partly coal-black world and partly too-blinding white—and he's in the middle, in a halfway kingdom, commanding everything.

He remains there under the branches until the sun sets, but he's never bored. He's used to doing things without haste. The whole trip is slow, and it gives him a chance to calmly watch the landscape slip by from up close. He observes the sky, where the clouds chase after one another, shifting their shadows over the objects below; and at eye level, the fields, which stretch out until they become hills beyond which he can see no farther. When evening falls, his mother gets the cheese out of the baskets. They eat together and chat, and the dinner ends with oranges and bananas, all gathered by the side of the road. Then weariness descends upon them all, and the group falls peacefully asleep.

At age fifteen, Sebastião leaves the farm to finish high school in Vitória, in the state of Espírito Santo. He's one of the first boys to move to the city to study. He pays his tuition by working in the secretarial pool of the Alliance Française, an agency that promotes French language and culture overseas, and he discovers that he actually has a fair aptitude for handling money. He then enrolls in law school, more than anything else to make his father happy—the old man wants him to become a lawyer. But truth be told, matters of the law bore Sebastião to death. He far prefers studying history and economics, subjects that help him understand the real world around him. This period, in fact, is a time of great transformation for Brazil, a country striving to become a modern industrial power under its new president. This whiff of progress infects Sebastião, too. Nonetheless, the prevailing atmosphere of joy and "everything's possible" slowly gives way to burgeoning new problems.

In the Brazilian countryside, as on the Salgado family's farm, the population is not divided between the super-rich and the terribly poor, and everyone has enough to get by.

In the Brazilian countryside, as on the Salgado family's farm, the population is not divided between the super-rich and the terribly poor, and everyone has enough to get by. In the cities, though, people crowd together in search of work in the factories, and the wealthy are blind to the inequality, though the streets overflow with the homeless and penniless.

Less than ten years later, the situation spirals out of control. A military coup d'état overthrows the legitimate government and sets up a dictatorship. This marks the beginning of a period of social upheaval and mass protests against totalitarian rule. Many young people, Sebastião among them, become opposition activists, leftist militants striving to defend the people and their rights.

In the meantime, having given up on becoming a lawyer, Sebastião changes his major to business. At the Alliance Française, where he has continued working, he meets Lélia, a young teacher, and falls head over heels in love with her. He gets his degree in 1967, and the next day, he marries Lélia.

The tension in Brazil continues to grow, and the dissidents, all those who are fighting against the regime, are increasingly at risk. And so Sebastião and Lélia leave the country and set off for Paris, and from there they continue to support the struggle for freedom, organizing

He starts taking pictures, and he never stops.

181

resistance groups and welcoming those fleeing Brazil's dictatorship. In France, they also resume their studies. Lélia enrolls in the Académie des Beaux-Arts, or "Academy of Fine Arts," while Sebastião, to make ends meet, spends his days working on a doctorate in economics and his nights as a stevedore.

Lélia buys a camera for one of her university classes. Sebastião has never held a camera in his life until then, but he immediately falls in love with it and buys two more lenses.

He starts taking pictures, and he never stops.

He's really good. For a pittance, he takes pictures of students and sells small photo essays about Brazilian authors to newspapers and magazines. He gradually makes up

And the more time that passes, the more he prefers taking pictures to writing.

his mind to become a professional photographer.

In the meantime, he gets a job as an economist at the International Coffee Organization, headquartered in London. He is responsible for starting economic development plans. His first assignment is in Africa, to start a project with support from the World Bank and the

UN Food and Agriculture Organization. Wherever he goes, he takes pictures.

"We're going to introduce tea cultivation in Rwanda," he tells Lélia in a long-distance phone call; she has remained behind in Paris to finish her studies. "That will give the country's economy new opportunities for growth, unlike now, when they're utterly dependent on coffee."

Sebastião falls in love with Africa. He is happy to see the same kind of vegetation he remembers from Brazil and the same colors as on his old plantation. He always has a camera hanging from a strap around his neck, and the more time that passes, the more he prefers taking pictures to writing economic reports.

"Let's change our lives," Lélia tells Sebastião when he returns home. "Forget about everything else and just focus on photography, pursue your overriding passion."

It is 1973. Sebastião stops working as an economist and becomes a photographer. He and Lélia invest all their savings in equipment and set out for their first reporting project, in his beloved continent of Africa. Sebastião takes pictures, while Lélia takes care of printing his work and selling the photographs to magazines.

The first picture she sells is a backlit shot of a woman standing next to a tree with a pitcher of water on her head. Sebastião took this picture with great confidence, even though backlit shots are a daunting challenge for any photographer. But he knows this blazing, excessive light all too well. He feels as if he can see his own parents under that tree, or herding their cattle. The picture is spectacular, and soon it is the talk of France. It is put up in poster form in every church in the country for the humanitarian campaign La Terre est à tous. Soon enough, Sebastião Salgado's name becomes well known. Sebastião joins a photo agency and starts traveling the world, reporting on the biggest news of those years.

"Did you hear that, Sebastião, they've issued an amnesty for all dissidents. We can finally go home to Brazil!" Lélia exclaims joyously one day while watching a news report on TV. Soon enough, they're both back home. They immediately head to the family farm, but their arrival is an enormous disappointment. Sebastião notices that much of the flora he remembers from his childhood has vanished. The trees have been cut down. The wood was used to build houses in the boom years, when he first moved to the city, and to provide charcoal for industrial manufacturing. The poverty he encounters in the surrounding areas is even more upsetting. Many farmers have sold their land at bargain prices to major corporations, and now they are forced to live unemployed, on the edges of what were once their own fields. In order to reclaim their rights, the farmers found the Landless Workers Movement and occupy the large landowners' untilled farmland; the landowners often fight back with great violence. Sebastião is struck by the peasants' determination. He photographs them and publishes a book to tell their story, prompting a surge in international solidarity. With his pictures, he simultaneously makes clear which side he's on and denounces the brutality of society and the harshness of life.

After spending years shoulder to shoulder with the courageous farmers of Brazil, Sebastião has the idea of staging a major photographic show paying homage to human beings' work and creativity. For more than ten years, from China and Indonesia to Cuba and Italy, he takes portraits of people busy creating things through their know-how, and he offers visual testimony of the conditions of workers, from the construction sites and factories of major industry all the way down to mines and quarries. The traveling exhibition is called *Workers: An Archaeology of the Industrial Age*, and it is shown around the world throughout 1993.

In 1994, with Lélia, he founds Amazonas Images, a photo agency, and begins work on *Migrations: Humanity in Transition*. "I still want to talk about human beings and their strength, about how they move en masse to flee wars and famines, but also in pursuit of the mirage of better jobs," he confides to Lélia. For six years, Sebastião travels from India to Brazil to Iraq. Everywhere he goes, he takes pictures of modern megalopolises and desperate

"I still want to talk about human beings and their strength, about how they move en masse to flee wars and famines, but also in pursuit of the mirage of better jobs."

slums where millions of people crowd together in search of work. All these people, far from their homelands, are adrift in an ocean of poverty and misery dotted by islands of super luxury for the privileged few.

The *Migrations* project also takes him to Mozambique, where civil war is pushing thousands of people into refugee camps in Malawi, Zimbabwe, and South Africa. After the war ends, Sebastião helps UNICEF and the World Health Organization reunite the families ripped apart by the conflict, photographing the faces of children and adults who've lost touch with their loved ones. From Mozambique, he goes directly to Rwanda, where vast rivers of people are flowing to Tanzania in search of safety.

"In Rwanda, a huge and unprecedented genocide is under way," Sebastião tells Lélia that night on the phone. "A bloodbath: corpses floating on the water like leaves, mountains of bodies piled up on the ground . . . the most horrifying war I've ever witnessed. I can't believe that this is the same country I got to know in the seventies," he concludes, appalled. After Rwanda's population boomed disproportionately, the resulting poverty created growing rifts between the two principal ethnic groups, the Hutus and the Tutsis, and the powder keg finally exploded, to disastrous effect.

"All the death and violence I witnessed while I was shooting *Migrations* shocked me deeply. I just don't know what kind of creature human beings are anymore. I took my pictures to give a voice to injustice, but I don't know if I'll be able to go on doing it," he confesses uneasily to Lélia once he returns home.

"Take some time off, Sebastião" she replies with profound understanding. "We could go back to your parents' plantation. We can plant trees, given that nearly all the trees are gone now. It would be good for the land

> "I took my pictures to give a voice to injustice, but I don't know if I'll be able to go on doing it."

and for us."

He loves the idea. Once they reach the farm, though, they realize that the situation is actually far worse than they remembered. Due to the lack of trees, rainwater no longer accumulates, and the soil has become as arid as a desert. What's more, of the many peasants who once worked on the farm, only a single watchman is left.

With the help of an engineer who specializes in eco-systems, they launch a project to restore the native flora and fauna by planting 2.5 million indigenous trees. In the fall of 1999, they sow the first seeds. By the following summer, shoots, seedlings, and saplings are already sprouting and blooming, and a tender green carpet starts to spread over the arid expanse, summoning insects to pollinate it. To finance the project, Sebastião and Lélia invest most of their money and seek aid from a number of environmental groups. The federal government even lends a hand. Before long, a miracle has taken place.

The land of Sebastião's childhood becomes Brazil's first national park, and today the family farm, now called Instituto Terra, is a nursery that provides over a million plants a year to the surrounding regions.

"It's even more beautiful than when I was a boy! You were right, Lélia. Only the beauty of the land could heal my heart," Sebastião says, embracing his wife after planting a new seedling.

The land of Sebastião's childhood becomes Brazil's first national park.

"It would be fantastic if we could tell this story, too," Lélia replies with a smile. She knows perfectly well that, in the end, Sebastião has to go back to his photography.

"We could create a new photographic narrative that captures the enchantment of nature. It may be true that humanity has destroyed half the planet, but it's every bit as true that a great deal of the world remains intact, and I want to immortalize it!" Sebastião concludes, his enthusiasm recovered.

This leads to the *Genesis* project, thirty-two reporting sessions dedicated to unspoiled landscapes, ranging from vast, icy territories to immense deserts and from tropical areas to arid zones. Sebastião's gaze adapts itself as he listens, sensing life in nonhuman forms, discovering much that is magnificent and deeply moving. From the Himalayas to the Galapagos, from New Guinea to Madagascar, Sebastião plunges into a wonderland of animals, plants, and land, and once again, he feels at peace.

THE LITTLE STORY OF
BJÖRK

I am Birch

jörk is motionless, eyes shut in the dazzling light of the Icelandic springtime. She digs her toes into the grass, balances on her left leg, and clasps both hands over her head.

"Do I look like a tree?" she asks her paternal grandmother, who is sitting at her easel.

"You *are* a tree!" her grandmother replies, as she smiles and puts down her paintbrush. *Björk* means "birch" in Icelandic.

The little girl abandons her pose and throws herself into her grandmother's open arms.

"I have to go now," Björk says, and she puts on her red ankle boots and is gone before you know it. She wants to go see her mother in the hippie commune in Reykjavík, a place where lots of friends live together, sharing everything. Björk is five years old; her parents are divorced. She has more than one home: sometimes she lives with her mother, sometimes with her father, and occasionally with her grandparents. She gets around on her own—her house keys hang on a chain around her neck—and is fearless.

As is so often the case in Iceland, it starts to rain without warning. The gust of icy water slaps her cheeks, but she loves the rain and cranes her head to feel the drops on her skin. Before catching the bus, she takes another stroll around the houses, in the moss-covered fields. Jumping from one puddle to the next, she sings at the top of her lungs. *I'll stay here a little longer*, she tells herself.

Surrounded by the sounds of nature, she feels her ideas settle down and grow orderly, lined up like elongated clouds.

Surrounded by the sounds of nature, she feels her ideas settle down and grow orderly, lined up like elongated clouds.

Back at the commune, though, there's such a tangle of words and music that her ears feel like they're on fire. The residents listen to Deep Purple and Jimi Hendrix at full volume, along with the classical music of Tchaikovsky.

Once she's completely calmed down, Björk returns to the main road, catches a bus, and goes to her mother's place.

The next morning, Björk gets back on the bus and returns to her father's home, where she lives with him and his mother, the grandmother who paints as a hobby. Her grandmother is making a *skyr* cake—*skyr* is a kind of fermented cheese that is said to date back to the ancient Vikings. Björk hugs her grandmother tight and gives her father a kiss, as he focuses intently on a report for his job. Then, tossing her ankle boots to the floor, she sits down at the piano. In a matter of minutes, her fingers are running over the black and white keys as she confidently plays a traditional song, singing along to it.

"It's incredible," her grandmother says to her father. "We heard it on the radio yesterday for the very first time, and Björk already plays perfectly. She really does have a gift for music."

"That's true. She was singing before she could talk," her father exclaims. "What do you say we send you to the conservatory next year?" he continues, speaking to his daughter.

Björk is delighted at the idea: "Thanks, Papa! That way I can perform all the time, not just on the bus or at home when people come over."

And so, at age six, Björk begins studying classical piano and flute in Reykjavík. After her daily lessons, she is free to choose where to spend the afternoon. She still has the keys to her home on a chain around her neck. She goes out for long, silent walks with her grandmother. When they get to the place where there is nothing but meadows and rocks, she sits down and makes up songs while the sun peeks out from behind the clouds. Other times, she wanders the countryside with her mother, who teaches her to fly the kites they make together.

"We're free, Björk, just like the wind," her mother tells her one day. And the little girl nods. *I can go wherever I want, just like the air*, she muses, as her eyes watch the twists and turns of her red paper diamond on a string.

In the meantime, Björk's musical talent grows. At age ten, she performs her version of a world-famous pop song at a school concert. Her teachers are so impressed with the quality and originality of her version that they take a recording of it to an Icelandic radio station. Her performance becomes a hit with the public, and before long, Björk is signing a recording contract with Fálkinn Records.

> "It's weird! The radio is sort of like the wind: it carries my voice everywhere."

"What's it like to hear yourself on the radio?" her mother asks her.

"It's weird! The radio is sort of like the wind: it carries my voice everywhere," the little girl replies, winking. Her almond-shaped green eyes earned her the nickname "China Girl" at school.

BJÖRK

"I think you'll go far, Björk," her mother tells her very seriously.

"Icelanders can't go far away from their island! We're a tiny dot lost in the Atlantic Ocean!" Björk says jokingly. Then she runs out the door and loses herself in the countryside. She doesn't even come in when it starts to snow. With her eyes wide open, she watches the flakes fluttering around her as the sound of silence envelops everything.

> "That landscape was sacred, and it filled me with a strength I'd never felt before. A perfect freedom."

When she turns thirteen, Björk shaves off her eyebrows and becomes a punk. She embraces a rebellious and provocative style of music, too, like the kind she heard at the commune. She tries out for a number of bands; in 1981, she joins a group called Exodus. They land a recording contract that allows her to earn a little money. She uses that money to buy a tent, and one morning, she sets out hitchhiking, without any exact destination. About sixty miles away from Reykjavík, she comes to a geyser, a jet of water that issues at irregular intervals from a circular hole in the ground, huffing, noisy, and massively powerful. Björk is hypnotized by it, and she starts singing to the rhythm of the water, as if she were in a dialogue with the bowels of the earth.

"That landscape was sacred, and it filled me with a strength I'd never felt before. A perfect freedom. I was inside the earth, among the spouts of boiling water and the icy air. It's like a composition that's tragic and peaceful at the same time," she tells her father when she returns from her trip. And for the first time, she understands clearly that, to her, music is something indissolubly bound up with the natural forces of her homeland.

"I need to be alone, in a place where the only sound is the cracking of the ice and the voice of the incandescent lava flowing from the volcanoes."

When she is still very young, Björk marries the musician Thor Eldon, and together they found the band the Sugarcubes. Their album *Life's Too Good* gives them a first taste of success and fame. Although Björk and Thor are soon divorced, the Sugarcubes stay together as a group until 1992. The following year, Björk finds worldwide success when *Debut*, her first solo album, comes out, garnering international prizes such as the MTV Video Music Award.

At the age of thirty-one, Björk is a full-fledged star living in London, in search of new sounds and collaborating with the most brilliant artists of the moment. Unfortunately, she discovers that being a celebrity has its disadvantages. The police intercept a package sent to her containing acid. A mentally unbalanced man has sent it with the intention of injuring her. Björk is profoundly shocked. She decides to leave London and go back to Iceland.

"I got a house on a mountaintop, where no one is going to be able to find me," she tells her mother.

"I need to be alone, in a place where the only sound is the cracking of the ice and the voice of the incandescent lava flowing from the volcanoes."

Back in her homeland, Björk goes out walking for hours on end. She sings in the open air the way she did when she was a girl, her voice resonating against the elements, and slowly she feels her strength return. Wild nature restores her and inspires her. One day, surrounded by the sounds of cracking ice and the now-cool solidified lava crunching under her feet, she thinks, *That's a truly techno sound. I need to make a song*

For an instant, Björk falls silent, breathless. She thinks back to the happy days of her childhood in nature and how it comforted her after the unsuccessful attempt on her life.

out of it. She returns home and starts recording immediately. The result is *Homogenic,* an album rife with
dissonance, violins, and electronica. It's immensely
popular. With her music, she also rediscovers her will
to get in the game: she stars in the film *Dancer in the
Dark* and wins the Palme d'Or for Best Actress at the
Cannes Film Festival.

"Our government is trying to manage a serious economic downturn. To get out of it, it's offering big international corporations permission to build enormous
aluminum smelting plants, which is endangering Iceland's ecosystem," her father tells her one day over the
phone, knowing full well how passionately Björk loves
her island.

For an instant, Björk falls silent, breathless. She thinks
back to the happy days of her childhood in nature and
how it comforted her after the unsuccessful attempt
on her life.

"I've always thought that music shouldn't have anything to do with politics, but Iceland is a small island,
with a population of a little over three hundred thousand. I have to do something for my homeland," she tells
her father. She decides to face some exposure, appear-
ing at the Hætta Festival, organized in Reykjavík. There
she protests the construction of a third factory by the
American company Alcoa, which would have turned
Iceland into Europe's largest foundry.

BJÖRK

The protest becomes part of her music. Her new album, *Volta*, is built around the theme of unspoiled nature. The phrase "the beast is back," from the song "Vertebræ by Vertebræ," announces that the beast— that is, nature—has returned to take back control of the planet and remind humans that they are only temporary guests. And the song "Earth Intruders" describes human beings as violent invaders bent on exploiting the earth and bending it to their will. The message is clear.

All the same, Björk still has faith that humans can change, and for a whole year she encourages Icelanders to take back their future. She founds the organization Náttúra to promote alternative forms of industry that do not harm the environment. She devotes herself completely to the new project: she visits rural areas and meets a great many people. "In a small town of five hundred souls, where twenty people are out of work, all it would take is two or three small businesses to make sure everyone had a job. You shouldn't think that it's better to work in a steel mill just because a large corporation can hire you all at a single blow. . . . Instead, you could till the soil and sell vegetables, or else start a service industry company or do online commerce," she tells them with great conviction.

She also raises funds to support new sustainable business practices and organizes meetings with businesspeople who respect the environment, urging them to set positive examples that may serve as inspiration. These encounters are a smashing success, and soon, lots of start-ups spring up around Iceland, employing over two thousand people in the most surprising of jobs.

Björk summarizes the ideas behind her commitment in an article she writes for the British newspaper the *Times*. She writes about the economic crisis sweeping Iceland, indicating that the only way of overcoming it is the sustainable deployment of natural resources.

The government, in the meantime, does its best to ignore the activists and continues its privatization of natural resources. For instance, it offers virtually total control of Icelandic geothermal energy for 130 years to the Canadian company Magma Energy.

In response, Björk launches a clear appeal on the pages of a major national newspaper: "Mr. Prime Minister, you must do everything within your power to cancel the contracts you've signed with Magma Energy." Then she starts a petition and organizes a three-day karaoke marathon to gather the signatures needed to call a referendum to halt the deal. Forty-seven thousand people sign the petition, which Björk then delivers to the prime minister in the form of a file on a USB flash drive. She doesn't even waste a single sheet of paper! The head of the government acts as if he's happy to receive it, but the situation remains unchanged.

Björk plunges back into nature, turning away from her public life for a while. After all her battles, she needs a new source of inspiration. Walking at dawn one morning in the silent Icelandic countryside, she realizes that ever since she was a little girl, it's always been the powerful energy of this land that has stunned her, giving her peace and strength at the same time. *It is precisely this astonishment that has always led me to love and respect this land. If only other people felt the same emotions, they'd understand,* Björk muses. This is the beginning of the creation of *Biophilia* (which means "love of life"), an innovative project that includes an album, a documentary, and an array of apps. The album's sound quality unites music, nature, and technology. As for the apps—they lead the listener to a multimedia exploration of the universe and its physical forces, but also contain educational games that teach sustainability and harmony among humans and other living species.

> Ever since she was a little girl, it's always been the powerful energy of this land that has stunned her, giving her peace and strength at the same time.

Iceland's natural resources continue to tempt the many interests eager to exploit them. In 2015, the British prime minister, David Cameron, visits the island.

He wants to undertake a project to build the world's longest underwater electric power cable (over fifteen hundred kilometers) in order to send part of the electricity generated by Icelandic geothermal plants to the United Kingdom. The project, however, requires an increase in the production of electricity, which would mean the construction of new electric power plants and numerous dams in the Highlands region. The Highlands of Iceland are a genuine natural treasure, home to such unique creatures as the pink-footed goose and the North Atlantic salmon. This precious environment, abounding in volcanoes, glaciers, rivers, waterfalls, geysers, and lava fields, would surely be devastated in just a matter of years by such a massive intervention. Once again, Björk feels called upon to defend her island.

"Iceland has Europe's largest unspoiled natural heritage, and the government's plan would lead to its destruction. This attack on the environment is not just a threat to us Icelanders, but also to all the inhabitants of the planet," she explains to the journalists in heartfelt tones. "We must create a national park in the Highlands. We need everyone's support to fight against

> This attack on the environment is not just a threat to us Icelanders, but also to all the inhabitants of the planet."

our government!" she adds, launching an appeal to the whole world.

If an agreement is worked out between the United Kingdom and Iceland, the construction of the Icelink, the underwater electric cable, could be carried out in the next few years. In the meantime, the initiative begun by Björk continues. Hálendið, Iceland's national park, in fact, has received the support and donations of private individuals and a great number of nature organizations.

"Nature has no lawyers of her own," Björk insists every chance she gets. "We must defend her because we are part of her," she concludes with a smirk on her face, and she thinks, *I know this . . . because I am Birch!*

THE LITTLE STORY OF MA JUN

For a swim in the yellow river

ittle Jun stares at the fishing pole. He's motionless. That afternoon, there are no fish willing to take the bait. The night before, he went hunting for insects hovering around the streetlamps near his house, and now he has a can filled to the brim with flying ants, butterflies, and spiders to use as bait. He tries switching bait, hooking a new insect and casting his line back into the canal. Then he patiently waits. The air in Beijing is hot and muggy. All around him he can hear the frogs croaking. His two friends, a few yards away from him, are also holding their fishing poles low.

"So, what if we went for a swim?" one of them asks.

In an instant, the fishing poles fly into the air, and the boys jump straight into the water. They swim with great agility, avoiding the stand of reeds, and in a few strokes, they're swimming upstream. When they get tired out, they swim back to shore and return to their fishing. At that point, Jun pulls his favorite book out of his bag and starts reading.

"Again?" one of his friends asks.

"Poetry takes time, just like fishing," Jun replies without even looking up from the page.

His friend glances at him, unconvinced. The boy doesn't like reading, and if he weren't obliged to do so at school, he'd be wary of so much as picking up a book.

"What's it about?" his other friend asks, curious now.

"About the Yellow River running down to the sea," Jun replies, his face lighting up.

"It must be a mighty river . . . They say that when it rains, it becomes a raging fury," his friend comments.

"It's one of the world's longest rivers, and it's the second-longest river in China," Jun clarifies. He is eight years old and has a full-blown obsession with large rivers. "It runs south of Beijing, and when I grow up, I plan to go see it. My parents say they'll let me."

At sunset, the boys collect their fishing poles and bait boxes and head home, without fish. That evening, Jun dreams of plunging into the crystal-clear waters of the Yellow River and emerging with dozens of carp.

"Papa, is it true that one of the tributaries of the Blue River creates waterfalls almost three hundred feet high and that behind them there's an enormous hidden grotto?" Jun asks at breakfast as soon as his father enters the kitchen.

"Jun, at least wish me good morning first!" the man replies, patting him on the cheek. "Anyway, it's true," he adds, touched.

Jun's father is an engineer, and whenever he's home, he conscientiously answers all his son's countless questions about the geography of China, an immense country. If there's something he doesn't know, he pulls out a map and spreads it out on the table. Then, together, they seek out mountains, rivers, and cities. Meanwhile, Jun's mother, an accountant, teaches Jun to move easily through the world of numbers.

"Count your change carefully before leaving the shop," she reminds him when she sends him out to buy something. "And be cautious."

The truth is that Jun was born cautious. He studies passionately and reads incessantly. "You'll become either a professor or a journalist," his friends always tell him. And in fact, at age twenty-four, in Beijing, Jun gets his degree in international relations with a specialty in journalism. He is immediately hired by the *South China Morning Post* as an investigative reporter with expertise in environmental topics.

Thanks to his job, Jun visits every corner of China. He discovers that what were once earthly paradises of unspoiled nature are now becoming progressively degraded wastelands.

Thanks to his job, Jun visits every corner of China. He discovers that what were once earthly paradises of unspoiled nature are now becoming progressively degraded wastelands.

"Agricultural and industrial businesses aren't sanctioned or punished in any way for the ecological damage they cause to rivers and lakes. They also aren't given an incentive to develop technologies for recycling water . . . though, nowadays, more than three hundred million people have no access to water resources," a worried Jun confides to his father, briefing him on his latest research findings.

Jun has witnessed firsthand that water pollution is China's most serious environmental problem because it causes damage to the health of ordinary people. With the economic boom of the past thirty years, the pollutants emitted by industry and households have increased to a dizzying degree, and the use of chemical fertilizers in agriculture has intensified. Sixty percent of China's rivers and lakes are covered by a carpet of algae, and the water is undrinkable; what's more, 90 percent of the city's water table is contaminated.

At age thirty-one, Jun collects his horrifying discoveries in a book, *China's Water Crisis*. In it, he describes the problems of pollution and the water shortages threatening communities, the economy, and the environment of China's seven biggest river basins. He also proposes solutions for a more sustainable future. Jun focuses on the Yellow River, which by this point has an insufficient flow in North China. He also describes the deforestation and excessive presence of dams along the Blue River and the dire droughts plaguing the cities in the country's southeast.

"In your book, I read that human activities are causing a dramatic reduction of the water flow in our two most important rivers, the Yellow River and the Blue River," his father tells him one evening at dinner over a steaming-hot plate of white rice and stewed green cabbage.

> "Full access to accurate information helps us understand that everyone can contribute to the solution."

"The Yellow River is at risk of disappearing! And the Blue River experiences alternating periods of drought and violent flooding!" Jun replies, waving his chopsticks in the air as if mimicking the rage of the current.

"The coming decades are going to be crucial in terms of solving the shortage of clean water. It's important that the Chinese know about every aspect of the problem. Full access to accurate information helps us understand that everyone can contribute to the solution," Jun continues, handing his mother a bowl of sweet and sour pork.

Jun is right, and yet he can't even imagine how right he is! His reporting rattles the public, and for months, no one talks about anything else. His articles travel around the world. *Time* magazine writes, "Ma Jun's 1999 book *China's Water Crisis* may be for China what Rachel Carson's *Silent Spring* was for the U.S.—the country's first great environmental call to arms."

"There are no more insects for fishing, and the river's beauty has vanished."

Jun is appointed editor of the Beijing bureau of the *South China Morning Post*. Out the window of his new office, he observes the city teeming with life and expanding furiously.

"There was a time when a car went by every ten minutes, but now the traffic flows past without stopping. There are no more insects for fishing, and the river's beauty has vanished. I wouldn't dive in for all the money in the world!" he tells his friend and assistant, Bo, as they head out to look into a new lead.

"Fishing here would be suicide. The fish absorb the toxic substances present in the river," Bo agrees, opening the car door.

They spend a few days in a small city in the south, where they investigate a case of industrial pollution.

Ma Jun

They notice that the vegetation in the countryside looks unwell. They decide to investigate. They park on a dirt road and start walking toward an old house where a peasant is sitting in a doorway coughing loudly. While Bo takes pictures, Jun chats with the man.

"I don't know what happened, but at a certain point we started feeling sick. Nausea, vertigo," the peasant tells him. "The grass along the riverbanks just suddenly turned yellow and dried up. We saw dead fish bobbing on the surface, and we understood something very serious was happening."

Jun has the peasant take him down to the river. He studies the water, sniffs it, and takes a sample in a test tube. Then he looks up and spies in the distance two menacing-looking structures upstream along the river.

"How long has it been since you first noticed a change in the water?" Jun asks, beginning to grasp the extent of these recent developments.

"A few months. We don't know what to do. We live on this land. Can you help us?"

Jun looks down for a moment, then raises his eyes and says, "We'll investigate in depth. Whoever caused all this won't get away with it."

As he's driving home, Jun is sad and angry. This isn't the first time that people have asked for his help. At the newsroom, too, he receives a great many letters that make him feel helpless.

The only thing that I can do is fight to make sure the people know. There is a need for greater transparency.

I don't have the money or power necessary to win a one-man environmental battle, he thinks. *The only thing that I can do is fight to make sure the people know. There is a need for greater transparency.*

In 2004, Jun is chosen by the World Fellows Program for his work in environmental research. Every year, sixteen people from different backgrounds and every part of the planet are invited to Yale University to work together "to make the world a better place." For four months, the researchers share data and experiences. Jun is delighted. While he's in the United States, he completes a study comparing U.S environmental policies with their Chinese counterparts and analyzing the way the two countries' environmental resources are managed. This is a very illuminating period.

Upon his return to China, Jun, in a series of articles, outlines the conclusions he reached during his period of research. In these pieces, he lists conservation proposals and pollutant alternatives to tackle the problem of water pollution.

"All the things I've learned have given me a crazy idea," he says one morning to his trusted Bo.

"I'm all ears," Bo replies, curious now, lifting his fingers from the keyboard.

"I want to create an online platform to report companies that pollute. First of all, I want to focus on the poisoning of drinking water sources. I have it all in my head," he announces.

Jun often clashes with people, from the factory owners who've done untold damage to those who've shown utter indifference when they should have been watching over those factory owners.

"To protect our water resources, we need everyone to get involved. It's not enough to tell people to obey the law. Citizens must be able to contribute to the monitoring of our waters, and the first step in involving them is to keep them informed!" he concludes.

The more the two colleagues talk, the more enthusiastic they become. They start planning and building the website. In May 2005 they begin uploading the data to the platform, but it's a monumental enterprise—there aren't enough hours in the day or night. So, they decide to involve two other friends, experts in the environment and computers, as well as several students.

This leads to the creation of the Institute of Public and Environmental Affairs (IPE), a nonprofit organization whose objective is to lessen the environmental impact of major industries in China through the publication of digital maps and reports identifying sources of pollution. The IPE aggregates, analyzes, and publishes environmental data supplied by government agencies, local administrations, and companies so that customers and citizens can get a clear picture of the health of the territories where they live. What's more, it supplies lists of virtuous companies and those that pollute, thus revealing that many multinationals in China are much less careful about environmental issues than they are in their home countries. If they know the truth, citizens can choose to purchase goods and services only from companies that adopt sustainable production systems.

"It's not enough to tell people to obey the law. Citizens must be able to contribute to the monitoring of our waters, and the first step in involving them is to keep them informed!"

"Serious, conscientious companies write to us saying that they're happy to be on the list, because the communities they work in place greater trust in their brand," Jun tells his coworkers with immense satisfaction.

Jun even comes up with an app, the Blue Map, that anybody can use to report cases of environmental pollution. This information is channeled through the IPE database to the proper authorities, who will then act to halt the abuses in question. He thus creates an effective tool for collaboration among citizens, the government, and all those who hope to comply with the law.

Jun receives a broad array of international awards. *Time* magazine includes him in its list "TIME 100: The Most Influential People of 2006." In 2012, he receives the Goldman Environmental Prize "for his work to protect the environment in China." In 2015, he is given a Skoll Award for Social Entrepreneurship "for his innovative approach in highlighting the problem of pollution in China."

Our children must be able to swim and fish in the rivers the way I did when I was a child, he thinks, dreaming once again of diving into the crystal-clear waters of the Yellow River.

Jun's enthusiasm and tireless investigations have led to a profound transformation in China. In 2016, China joined the Paris Agreement on Climate Change, committing to updating its plans for active measures to contain global warming below two degrees centigrade. Li Keqiang, premier of the People's Republic of China, recently even promised to "make Chinese skies blue again." Jun is optimistic, but he also knows that there is a great deal more work to be done.

"Nature is everyone's home, and only when society mobilizes as a whole can environmental degradation be halted," he says in one of the many lectures he delivers in China and around the world. *Our children must be able to swim and fish in the rivers the way I did when I was a child*, he thinks, dreaming once again of diving into the crystal-clear waters of the Yellow River.

THE LITTLE STORY OF
Yvon
Chouinard

A rebellious entrepreneur

"No, I'm not staying here!" Yvon says to his classmate before sneaking out of the classroom and vanishing into the fields behind the school. At age seven, he's already a genuine rebel. Ever since his family moved from Maine to California, traveling along Route 66, he's done nothing but skip class and escape into nature. His family enrolled him in a Burbank public school where only English is spoken, though he speaks only French. Yvon is the smallest kid in the class, and everyone makes fun of him because he has a French "girl's name."

After the umpteenth escape into the fields, his parents transfer him to a Catholic school. Here, too, Yvon is almost always alone, but he's never bored. In the afternoon, he bikes more than six miles to a lake on a private golf course, where he stealthily fishes for perch and bass. On one expedition, he discovers the oasis of Griffith Park, which borders the Los Angeles River. There he has even more fun: he swims; he throws rocks into the water; he constructs toy harpoons, traps, and snares to catch frogs and shrimp; or he hunts wild hares with a bow and arrow.

Like his father, who is a carpenter and a plumber, Yvon is capable of building everything he needs. He combines the things he finds in nature with scraps from his father's workshop. His mother would never dream of scolding him for his raids and hijinks, because she's convinced that nature teaches self-sufficiency. So, while other children his age aren't even allowed to cross the street on their own, Yvon explores the American wilderness from one end of the country to the other.

Yvon explores the American wilderness from one end of the country to the other.

In high school, Yvon remains a bit of a loner: shy and awkward at parties, though he's almost never invited to them in the first place. Even studying offers little solace: he gets bored in class, unless the subject is a practical one. While the teachers explain, he thinks about what he's going to do after school or he practices holding his breath so that he can remain underwater longer while hunting lobsters.

One morning, sick and tired of seeing him always looking out the window, his math teacher decides to punish

Yvon. He makes him sit in the back of the classroom and write five hundred times, "I will not get distracted during class." Stimulated by the challenge, Yvon uses rubber bands and pencils to make a triple-pencil writing device that allows him to write the sentence three times simultaneously.

In springtime, with other students who aren't especially interested in school, and with the help of a nonconformist teacher, Yvon organizes a falconry group.

"After we find the nests, we'll start training the young falcons to hunt," the teacher says.

At age fifteen, Yvon watches over the bird he's assigned for days on end, encouraging it to come closer. He talks to the young falcon in a calm voice and encourages it with morsels until the animal trusts him implicitly and falls asleep on Yvon's clenched fist. Being accepted by such a fierce bird fills Yvon with pride.

As he makes his way down from the rocks in search of another nest, he meets some climbers heading in the opposite direction. Thrilled, he decides to learn how to climb. He trains until he feels safe. That same weekend, he hops aboard a freight train heading for the San Fernando Valley. Once he reaches his destination, he jumps off the moving train and goes to climb the sandstone formation of Stoney Point. He doesn't have any money to buy equipment, so he ties a hemp rope (stolen from a phone company) around his shoulders and waist.

Yvon Chouinard

At age sixteen, in an old Ford he fixed up in shop class, he ventures with his friends to Wyoming and, farther still, to the Rocky Mountains. He climbs increasingly sheer ridges and peaks and indulges in a little fly-fishing in the lakes farther down.

After high school, Yvon attends university for two years, paying for his studies with a part-time job as a private investigator. Then, in the summer, with his skimpy savings, he explores the Mexican coast all the way to Mazatlán.

The next year, just as he did when exploring as a child, Yvon constructs his own climbing equipment. Now he's fairly experienced with steep slopes and the kind of unexpected emergencies that crop up when you're dangling over the void. He knows that tools have to be light and sturdy.

The gear is costly for him—it includes pitons that can be used only once, to remain there, pounded deep into the rock. Yvon loves the mountains and doesn't want to leave anything on the high ridges that doesn't belong there. So, he decides to make pitons that can be extracted and reused repeatedly. He buys everything he's going to need from a junkman: a one-hundred-pound anvil,

> Yvon loves the mountains and doesn't want to leave anything on the high ridges that doesn't belong there.

a kit of hammers and tongs, and a secondhand forge. And he is successful. Soon Yvon's handmade pitons capture the attention of friends and acquaintances, who buy them in bulk.

Demand for the pitons grows so fast that, with his father, Yvon repurposes the old hen house behind his family's Burbank home and sets up his first real workshop. Still, he's only eighteen years old, and he doesn't want to give up his freedom. So, he creates a mobile workshop and travels from beach to beach along the California coast, from Big Sur to San Diego. Every time he reaches a new destination, he does some surfing and then sets up shop at the water's edge, fabricating his super-sturdy pitons with anvil, hammer, and chisels.

The following year, he changes tack. In the winter, in Burbank, he prepares his pitons and carabiners. From April to July, he climbs the highest peaks of Yosemite and Canada and earns a living by selling the equipment he carries in his car, which also serves as his home away from home.

Strong and free like the animals among whom he lives in nature, Yvon feels light years away from modern society, which is continuing its relentless economic growth, producing objects and encouraging consumption and wealth at all costs. He isn't interested in money and success.

YVON CHOUINARD

In 1962, he's drafted into the military and winds up in South Korea. As soon as he's discharged, Yvon goes back to climbing the most challenging peaks in the world and trying out new versions of his equipment. He founds Chouinard Equipment, his first real company. His full-time employees are all fellow climbers. In 1966, to get closer to surfing territory, Yvon moves to Ventura County. He converts an old abandoned slaughterhouse into a factory and begins his career as a businessman, while still remaining a rebel at heart.

The day of the move, once all the machinery is installed and all the cartons are unpacked, he summons his entire staff. "To me, Chouinard Equipment is a family, a group of friends, and I want you all to be happy here," he says. "Your happiness interests me much more than profits. We all love to climb and to surf, and so our schedules are going to be flexible, so that we can get to the mountains and the beach. Have fun working!" His imaginative management style turns out to be successful, because all his employees are motivated and relaxed, and what's more, they are producing innovative equipment that they can use in the outdoor activities they love most.

Strong and free like the animals among whom he lives in nature, Yvon feels light years away from modern society.

In 1968, Yvon meets Malinda, a skilled climber; and in 1970 they get married. That same year, when Malinda joins the company, Chouinard Equipment becomes the leading supplier of climbing gear in the United States.

One afternoon, while out climbing, Yvon sees six large holes in a vein in the rock wall, one above the other, like six gaping wounds. He immediately understands that these are the marks left by his reusable pitons, and he is suddenly filled with shame. He examines alternative approaches and soon comes up with a set of aluminum chockstones that can be wedged into the rock without using a hammer, making use of natural cracks and fissures already present.

"Climbing with only nuts and runners for protection is clean climbing," Doug Robinson writes in the 1972 Chouinard catalogue. "Clean is climbing the rock without changing it; a step closer to organic climbing for the natural man."

The chockstones that do nothing to wound the mountain sell like hotcakes.

In the early 1970s, Yvon starts making athletic apparel and backpacks, venturing into a new enterprise, in search of fabrics that are light but strong. Sales are so strong that he has to start a second company. "I'll call it Patagonia, an exotic name that insinuates travel and mystery, easy to pronounce in all languages!" Yvon announces to Malinda, and she approves the choice with a smile.

Yvon Chouinard

One evening, Yvon is invited by a friend to a meeting of the city council to discuss a plan to develop the Ventura River. Ever since the construction of two dams reduced the flow of water, the river, once an ideal habitat for rainbow trout, has practically been reduced to a stagnant pool The technicians paid by the city believe that all animal life has vanished from the river and that they can therefore reroute its channel.

"Our river isn't dead at all!" a young biologist named Mark Capelli interrupts them forcefully, displaying photographs of animals in the water and on the riverbanks. "There are still mice, birds, snakes, eels, and even rainbow trout laying eggs in this river. Without the water, though,

> "Clean is climbing the rock without changing it; a step closer to organic climbing for the natural man."

they really will all die!" After hearing those words, the citizens reject the project, and the river is saved.

Yvon is very impressed by the biologist's courage. He lends him an office and underwrites his association for the defense and cleanup of the river. Soon, rainbow trout are flourishing and animal life is proliferating along the banks of the Ventura River.

"Mark has taught us two things," Yvon tells his coworkers. "First, that small groups of citizens can make a difference; and second, that even the most damaged and degraded habitats can be restored to health if we're willing to make the necessary effort."

Inspired by Mark's courage and results, Yvon starts to make personal donations and devote a regular share of his companies' profits to small associations fighting on behalf of environmental causes. Then, in 1988, Patagonia starts a national ecological campaign against the unbridled urban development of the Yosemite Valley. Many more campaigns in defense of the planet are to follow all over the world. Yvon and Malinda, in the meantime, try to limit the breakneck growth of their company, worried that excessive growth might hinder the quality of their production and the well-being of their employees. So, they decide not to sell their products in department stores and not to list their company's shares on the Stock Exchange. At the end of the eighties, they sell Chouinard Equipment and devote themselves to managing Patagonia alone. The latter company is doing very well indeed, thanks to innovative products made of pile, an ecological fabric manufactured from recycled plastic bottles.

When he comes back from one of his trips to the great outdoors, Yvon is very uneasy. He witnessed the effects of industrialization on the environment, the deforestation and the polluted rivers.

"The excess of consumption and manufactured products in modern society is slowly suffocating nature. Are we sure we want to go on being businessmen? Even our manufacturing produces waste and uses up resources," he confides in Malinda, worried now.

"We have to try to do as little damage as possible," she replies, every bit as worried as he is.

With that in mind, Yvon investigates the environmental impact of the four types of fibers used to produce his company's best-selling items. The result is shocking: the one that produces the most pollution is cotton. In fact, growing cotton requires pesticides and insecticides that poison land and water, and they're toxic for the workers, too.

"How can we go on manufacturing products with a fiber that is such an awful pollutant? Especially if we consider that just to make a T-shirt, we have to use three thousand liters of water. This is unsustainable madness!" he tells his coworkers, and they set out to come up with ecological alternatives. In 1994, he decides that within the next two years, Patagonia is going to produce garments made exclusively of organic cotton, grown without pesticides or herbicides; and to the extent the company is able, it's going to reduce its level

"The excess of consumption and manufactured products in modern society is slowly suffocating nature."

of water consumption. Patagonia does with its fabrics what Chouinard Equipment tried to do with its aluminum climbing chockstones.

Continuing to ask questions concerning the provenance and sourcing of its fabrics and their impact on the environment and the lives of its employees, Patagonia also introduces hemp, recycled polyester, and dyes and colorants free of all toxic substances. Yvon is proud that now his company's entire line of clothing consists of garments made from recyclable fabrics.

"Recycling is fundamental," Yvon tells his employees, "because these days, human beings are living beyond their means."

Yvon has chosen to be a rebellious entrepreneur, a businessman who defends at all costs both nature (rather than mere profit) and the happiness of his employees.

He remains committed to making his business increasingly sustainable by recycling paper; setting up solar panels on the roofs of his factories, plants, and warehouses; and organizing exhibits and press campaigns on the environment.

"Clothing and all manufactured objects in general must have as many lives as possible," he never tires of explaining during his training courses. Patagonia encourages its customers to repair their clothing; to bring garments into their stores to have them mended; or else, if they're too far gone, to begin their recycling process. He even goes so far as to urge his customers not to buy his products at all, unless they absolutely need them.

> Yvon has chosen to be a rebellious entrepreneur, a businessman who defends at all costs both nature (rather than mere profit) and the happiness of his employees.

"It's difficult to imagine an economy that satisfies all seven billion of us, yet doesn't destroy the earth. . . . Certainly, we should replace old inefficient and polluting technologies with less damaging and cleaner ones, but that does not solve the true problem: ever-expanding growth on a finite planet." As a child, when he fished in lakes with a pole and a hook, he felt that a simple life offered all that mattered. Now, while running one of the world's biggest companies, he's certain of it.

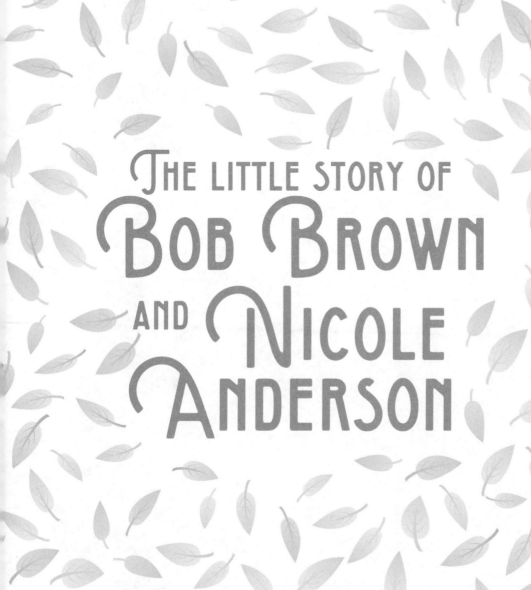

THE LITTLE STORY OF
BOB BROWN
AND NICOLE ANDERSON

There's room for dreamers and for wallabies

Bob Brown and Nicole Anderson

Bob carefully stacks the last stone on his shelter. He's been working on it for a week now, and it's finally done. That afternoon, even if it rains, he'll be able to stay in the woods and read. He loves being under the cover of the trees, and he never feels lonely. He churns through page after page. The frogs croak, the red-necked wallabies hop past, and Bob is at peace with the world. At lunchtime, he heads home, enjoying the bright colors of the fields around Trunkey Creek, the Australian village where he lives, once home to a wave of gold prospectors.

Bob studies the grass, in search of field mushrooms. His careful attention is soon rewarded.

"Look what I found!" he says, entering the kitchen, still panting with excitement. His T-shirt is now a bundle of mushrooms.

"Wow!" his mother exclaims. "We can eat them in a salad. Now go wash up. Your father will be home soon, and you know how he hates a mess."

Bob climbs into the tub, and half an hour later he's already sitting in the dining room, ready to eat. He nervously drums his feet under the table.

"Sit still at the table, Bob," his father says after a little while. His father is the town policeman.

"Sorry, it's just that I finished building the stone shelter today, and I have to hurry back to make sure it's still standing. It might have been invaded by wallaby cubs . . ."

"A stone house, built by a seven-year-old boy, invaded by wallaby cubs? Where do you come up with these things?" his father asks in amusement. "You really are a daydreamer!" he concludes cheerfully.

"Nature is full of variety. There's room for dreamers and for wallabies!" Bob retorts as he leaps out of his chair. Then he grabs an apple and hurries back to the woods.

At age sixteen, he moves to Blacktown, in Greater

> "Nature is full of variety. There's room for dreamers and for wallabies!"

Western Sydney, where he attends Blacktown Boys High School. At age twenty-four, he gets a degree in medicine in Sydney and starts working as a doctor at Royal Canberra Hospital. In those years, there's a terrible war raging between North Vietnam and the United

States. Australia supports the Americans and sends its own soldiers to fight. Bob, who dreams of a peaceful world, helps young men who want to avoid being sent to the front, refusing to supply them with the certificates of sound health that would oblige them to enlist.

He continues his practice of medicine in many other hospitals, and then, with a three-month employment contract in hand, he finally moves to Tasmania, an Australian island to the southeast of the country. Along the way from Launceston to the waterfalls of the Liffey River, he spots a white cottage surrounded by fields and forests and, next to it, a beautiful walnut tree. A sign says that the cottage is for sale.

"It's mine! I'll buy it!" he says to himself, and for eight thousand dollars, he buys the house with about twenty-five acres of woods and meadows. He calls it Oura Oura, the name of a character in an old Aboriginal legend. Here, for the first time in his life, Bob feels at home.

The wildlife in Tasmania stuns and enchants him: duck-billed platypuses, kangaroos, opossums, and snakes. Life

> The wildlife in Tasmania stuns and enchants him.

is everywhere, and it frequently flies in through the windows, wriggles under the doors, and gallops toward him while he's on his long walks through the woods, along rivers and torrents, or up into the mountains.

In the evening, he sits on the veranda reading or writing; he cooks outdoors; and sometimes he sleeps outside under the stars. During the week, he bikes for thirty miles to his clinic in Launceston. On Fridays, he returns to the cottage with plenty of supplies for the weekend. He talks for hours with his friends in the shade of a walnut tree, a place that has witnessed a great many important moments in his life.

One evening, a friend comes rushing in, breathless, and tells him that the ecosystem of the Franklin and Gordon Rivers is threatened by plans for a three-hundred-foot-tall dam intended to produce hydroelectric power. "We can't allow this paradise to be destroyed," Bob says, ready for the fight.

He joins the United Tasmania Group, the first green political party on earth, a handful of dreamers who bring environmental defense into the realm of politics. Then, with sixteen friends, in the shade of his beloved walnut tree, he founds the Tasmania Wilderness Society. The new organization calls for watchdog groups put in place along the riverbanks, meetings with the populace, and protest marches all over Australia. The controversy over the dam grows and spreads: twenty thousand people march in Hobart, the capital of Tasmania; another fifteen thousand demonstrate in Melbourne;

and equally large crowds march in Sydney, Canberra, and Adelaide. For the climax of the protest, Bob brings together thousands of activists to face off against the bulldozers, which stand ready to flatten and scrape the earth prior to the construction of the dam. His group's mass sit-in prevents the construction machinery from moving forward. Four hundred ninety-nine people, plus Bob, are thrown in jail.

"Dear Mother and Father, before being arrested, I thought about the two of you. It must be very hard for you to understand me sometimes. But I believe in what I'm doing, and so do my fellow protesters," he writes from his cell.

After nineteen days behind bars, including Christmas Eve 1982 and New Year's Day 1983, he is released. His courage is rewarded when, the next day, Bob is elected to Parliament as a representative from Tasmania and the candidate for the United Tasmania Group.

"After seven years of protests, the project for the dam is halted, and the ecosystem of the Franklin River and the Gordon River is saved. UNESCO adds it to the list of World Heritages sites, as part of the Tasmanian Wilderness World Heritage Area," Bob proudly announces to the journalists. Soon, thanks to his efforts, the list of areas safeguarded expands to include a protected area of about 2.5 million acres, roughly a fifth of Tasmania.

BOB BROWN AND NICOLE ANDERSON

But other battles await him. "The whole island must become a nature preserve," he tells the journalists. "Next comes Tarkine, the region that has been ninety percent ruined by open-pit mining."

Among all the territories of Tasmania, in fact, Tarkine (known as "Takayna," in Palawa kani, a composite Tasmanian language) is one of the most delicate and precious: over a million acres of land enclosed by the Arthur and Pieman Rivers and the coastline, with vegetation made up of species dating back sixty million years. It contains the largest temperate rainforest in Australia and boasts more than sixty protected species. According to samples taken by the Cape Grim Baseline Air Pollution Station, it also has the world's purest air. This is where the Aboriginal population originated. The island's ancient inhabitants, along with their thousand-year-old culture, are at risk of vanishing along with the nature that has always sheltered them.

"The government must invest in sustainable businesses that create new jobs," Bob proposes, ending the press conference.

The prime minister of Tasmania crushes his hopes: "We're going to keep on working as we always have. Let me be perfectly clear: as long as there's an ounce of tin left to mine, Tarkine won't become a national park.

These fanatical environmentalists are blowing its importance out of proportion!"

Many citizens who work in the mining or lumber industries agree with the prime minister because they're afraid of losing their jobs. Given the strength of their public support, the government begins more clear-cutting projects in the region: more trees that have taken hundreds of years to grow are felled in just a few minutes.

The activists meet in order to get organized. "The woodcutters are moving forward, clear-cutting everything they see. Then they set fire to the area, destroying the forest at the root," Bob explains to them. To prevent the felling of the trees, some of the activists climb onto the highest branches and live there for weeks. Bob visits one of them.

"How long have you been up there, Lisa?" he asks a

> "The government must invest in sustainable businesses that create new jobs."

young woman perched high up in a giant old tree.

"Three weeks," she replies.

"Thanks for what you're doing! If the twenty-five million Australians knew, they'd be grateful to you, too," he tells her.

"Sometimes it's tough, but it's meaningful to be up here. Every minute I spend here makes me feel closer to the forest," Lisa replies.

Bob puts apples and books in a basket for her.

"Thanks, I'll eat them this afternoon . . . and I'll have plenty to read for the rest of the week!" Lisa says as she pulls the basket up on a rope.

Bob comes up with new ways of removing uncontaminated areas from industry's intensive exploitation. In 1990, he establishes Bush Heritage Australia, which purchases land in order to transform it into nature reserves. For years he travels extensively to lecture on the consequences of the out-of-control consumption of wood resources and to motivate citizens to use their votes to stop the depletion. In the meantime, he organizes peaceful demonstrations to protect the unspoiled forests of Tarkine, which are threatened by the construction of new roads. In 1995, he is arrested twice more.

Thanks to his tireless work, ecological issues finally awaken interest among the voters: this marks the beginning of the first group of Australian Green parliamentarians. In 1996, Bob becomes their leader.

That same year, he meets Paul, the love of his life and a tireless supporter of his environmental battles.

Working in politics is often difficult and frustrating. One morning, to recharge his energy, Bob goes for a walk in the woods. He walks in silence, lost in thought. He breathes in the fresh air charged with the spores of fungi and ferns, and he immediately feels better.

Nature always brings us back to reality. Human beings have evolved for two million years in the natural environment. It's not the result of the last two hundred years of industrial civilization, he thinks.

Thanks to his tireless work, ecological issues finally awaken interest among the voters.

Heading down the same road, but in the opposite direction, is Nicole Anderson, a young doctor who loves to run alone through the rainforest.

"Hey! You're an athlete. I can't really run," Bob says by way of a greeting.

"I'm not really an athlete, to be honest. It's just something I do to explore places. I've only been here for a year," she says, running in place to maintain her pace. "It's just a matter of training. The human body is built especially for running: the thorax allows us to breathe deeply, ensuring we can hold out over long distances."

"Sounds to me like you're a doctor. Well, so am I. We're the only ones who would use that kind of terminology in casual conversation," Bob observes with an ironic smile.

Nicole smiles and stops running in place. "Yes, my office is in Smithton . . . but I run here every chance I get."

"Then why don't you run for us?" Bob asks her point blank.

"I don't know who 'us' refers to, but I'm not a professional athlete. I cover long distances, but I'm pretty slow," Nicole replies, baffled.

Bob invites her to his house for a chat in the shade of the walnut tree. Instinctively, Nicole trusts him and goes along.

"It's beautiful here. It reminds me of when I was a little girl. I would light a fire in my backyard and cook outdoors. I wanted to stay outside forever, though it drove everyone crazy. That's when I learned the first strategies of survival in the woods," Nicole recalls.

"I still do the same thing," Bob tells her, pointing at the charred pile of ashes close by. Then he turns serious and adds: "This wonderful place deserves respect." He goes on to tell her about the battles he and other activists have been waging to defend Tarkine and the thousand-year-old culture of the Aborigines.

"The government is actually shutting down as much as twenty miles of roads to conceal its clear-cutting of the native forest. That way it can work without hindrance," Bob explains.

"We have every right to know what's happening on public land!" Nicole says indignantly.

"That's why we need a lookout in Tarkine, someone who can keep an eye on the work the government is doing. Would you like to be our scout?" Bob asks her.

Nicole realizes that she has another important mission in Tasmania: "I'm with you!" she exclaims enthusiastically.

She takes pictures and finds points of access to allow the other environmentalists to climb the trees or take up positions in front of the bulldozers. Sometimes she has a hard time getting her bearings because, a few weeks before, these places became barren and unrecognizable. When she gets too sad, she turns to Bob.

"The work you're doing is essential, Nicole," Bob tells her seriously. "It helps us prove that the government is lying when it talks about sustainable deforestation. The fact that they might leave an ancient tree standing here

"They're crazy. Don't they know that we're part of the forests, just like our ancestors?"

"There's something unique in the primordial nature of this land. No scientist can reproduce it, no composer can rival it, no writer can describe it. I'm at peace."

or there doesn't change matters in the slightest. Without other trees like it, it will soon fall of its own accord, and there will be no trace left of the old forest."

"They're crazy. Don't they know that we're part of the forests, just like our ancestors? We're intertwined with nature in many different ways: genetically, physically, and biochemically, as well as emotionally and spiritually," Nicole says, more determined than ever to carry out her mission.

In 2011, after living in the white cottage for forty years, Bob donates his property to Bush Heritage Australia, which transforms the property into the Liffey Valley Reserves. Then he moves to Cygnet, to live with Paul, who is a farmer and owns a great deal of land and sheep. Tired of political life, Bob quits all his posts the following year, but he remains in contact with the other activists and in particular with Nicole. "You will help me keep track of Takayna's health. You can always count on me. Protecting the environment is my life," Bob tells her reassuringly. With that in mind, he establishes the Bob

Brown Foundation, which fights for UNESCO protection of new regions of unspoiled wildlife. The foundation's first initiative is the Nelson River Valley, which becomes a nature reserve in 2013. The Bob Brown Foundation also continues the fight to add Tarkine to the other protected sites, thus giving the land back to the Aborigines.

"Bob, we need to work fast, because the government intends to clear-cut one hundred fifty other areas. I've already seen them closing down roads," Nicole tells him one day, concern in her voice. Bob does his best, and in 2017 his labors begin to bear fruit when 835 acres of land along the Arthur River, better known as King's Run, are returned to the Aborigines.

"Without Nicole, we never could have done it. I want to go on dreaming of a better future for us all," he confides to Paul one evening. "There's something unique in the primordial nature of this land. No scientist can reproduce it, no composer can rival it, no writer can describe it. I'm at peace. Nicole's fighting spirit ensures the salvation of Tarkine."

CAROLA BENEDETTO is a Hindologist, author, and playwright. She codirected *Pierre Rabhi: Il mio corpo è la terra* (2013), the first Italian documentary about Rabhi, one of the leading figures in the field of agroecology. She wrote the afterword to Pierre Rabhi's *La sobrietà felice* (2013, Add Editore). She was the co-director of the festival, Per sentieri e remiganti, il Festival dei viaggiatori extra ordinari (2007–2014, Turin). With Luciana Ciliento, she wrote *La terra non è mai sporca* (2018, Add Editore) and has been a regular guest on the television shows Overland '19 (RAI 1) and Overland '20 (RAI 1).

LUCIANA CILIENTO is a translator and interpreter, as well as the co-director of the festival, Per sentieri e remiganti, il Festival dei viaggiatori extra ordinari (2007–2014, Turin). She translated the DVD *Pierre Rabhi: Il miocorpo è la terra*, and oversaw its presentation all over Italy. With Carola Benedetto, she wrote *La terra non è mai sporca* (2018, Add Editore) and has been a regular guest on the television shows Overland '19 (RAI 1) and Overland '20 (RAI 1).

ANTONY SHUGAAR is a writer and a translator from the Italian and the French. He has translated close to forty novels for Europa Editions, including his translation of *Hollow Heart* by Viola Di Grado, shortlisted for both the PEN and the ALTA Italian translation awards. He has received two National Endowment for the Arts fellowships.